# LETTERS  T

Bonhoeffer's previously unpublished
correspondence with Ernst Cromwell,
1935–6

## DIETRICH BONHOEFFER

Edited by Stephen J. Plant
and Toni Burrowes-Cromwell

Society for Promoting Christian Knowledge
36 Causton Street
London SW1P 4ST
www.spckpublishing.co.uk

Scripture quotations are from the New Revised Standard Version of the Bible,
Anglicized edition, copyright © 1989, 1995 by the Division of Christian Education of
the National Council of the Churches of Christ in the United States of America, and
are used by permission. All rights reserved.

The publisher acknowledges with thanks permission to reproduce the following:
Letters of Ernst Cromwell are taken from *Theological Education at Finkenwalde:
1935–1937*. Dietrich Bonhoeffer Works, Vol. 14, copyright © Fortress Press, admin.
Augsburg Fortress. Reproduced by permission. All rights reserved.
As of September 2013, publication of the letters in the original German is
forthcoming in the next issue of the *Dietrich Bonhoeffer Jahrbuch/Yearbook*,
published by Gütersloher Verlagshaus.
Every effort has been made to acknowledge fully the sources of material reproduced
in this book. The publisher apologizes for any omissions that may remain and, if
notified, will ensure that full acknowledgements are made in a subsequent edition.

*British Library Cataloguing-in-Publication Data*
A catalogue record for this book is available from the British Library

ISBN 978–0–281–06669–8
eBook ISBN 978–0–281–06670–4

Typeset by Caroline Waldron, Wirral, Cheshire
First printed in Great Britain by Ashford Colour Press
Subsequently digitally printed in Great Britain

eBook by Graphicraft Limited, Hong Kong

Stephen J. Plant is Dean and Runcie Fellow at Trinity Hall, University of Cambridge, where he teaches theology and ethics in the Divinity Faculty. He edited the journal *Theology* for SPCK from 2007 to 2013 and is the author of several books including *Taking Stock of Bonhoeffer: Studies in Biblical Interpretation and Ethics* (Ashgate Press, 2014).

Toni Burrowes-Cromwell is an International Development Specialist and former International Director of one of the UK's largest children's charities. Her background spans student ministry, social policy reform and programme delivery across the Caribbean, in southern Africa and in Canada. Toni is affiliated with several professional associations including the International Society for Third Sector Research (ISTR).

# LETTERS TO LONDON

# Contents

# Preface and acknowledgements

Though Dietrich Bonhoeffer is one of the most important theologians of the twentieth century, most of his fame came posthumously. When Ernst Cromwell met him in late 1934 or early 1935 Bonhoeffer was 29 years old and relatively unknown. Though by this stage Bonhoeffer was already actively resisting state interference in church life (and was one of a small number of Christians arguing that the Church had a responsibility to resist Nazism more widely by standing alongside innocent victims of state aggression and injustice), the young Ernst Cromwell was largely unaware of and uninterested in Bonhoeffer's background. The friendship they formed in the mid 1930s was, therefore, very simply that of pastor and confirmand and was unaffected by the fame (and notoriety) that would attach later to Bonhoeffer as a participant in the treasonous assassination attempt on Hitler of July 1944, or as the brilliantly original theologian who emerged from the publication *post mortem* of his prison letters. By the time war ended and news of Bonhoeffer's execution at Flossenbürg concentration camp on 9 April 1945 became public, Ernst Cromwell had moved on. His own experience of war intervened between him and Bonhoeffer, and he had his own life to get on with. He was well aware of Bonhoeffer's growing fame, but felt disinclined to contribute to the chatter by drawing attention to Bonhoeffer's role in his own formation. Fully naturalized as an Englishman and after 1941 with an Anglicized first name, Ernest Cromwell, like most others of his generation, valued privacy, both his own and Bonhoeffer's.

In the autumn of 2010, during a house refurbishment, Ernest's son Andrew rediscovered a number of letters written to his father by Bonhoeffer in 1935 and 1936. The letters had been kept carefully and deliberately, interleaved in a number of books. Now approaching his ninetieth birthday, Ernest Cromwell asked Toni Burrowes-Cromwell (his daughter-in-law) to assume responsibility for them due to the keen interest she had had in Bonhoeffer since her teenage years. In November 2010 Toni invited Stephen Plant to see the cache of letters. It was plain to them both that the letters ought to be in the public domain; the volume you are reading is the outcome of a process to make the letters available in print.

This volume is clearly not an introduction to Bonhoeffer's life and thought; for that, one may choose from one of several accessible introductions currently in print.[1] What the letters published in this volume give is a densely pixellated snapshot of Bonhoeffer in sharp focus at a particular moment and in a particular pastoral relationship. Here we can see Bonhoeffer in the period when he prepared to leave congregational ministry in London to take up a post as director of a seminary training ministers for the illegal Confessing Church. These letters and the photographs accompanying them are a significant new find that add colour and texture to our knowledge of what is going on at a comparatively neglected period. In them we see Bonhoeffer pulled between his various callings to pastoral ministry, theological teaching and political resistance. We see him trying on religious community life for size, squeezing out time to travel from a busy schedule, and reflecting on friendships lost and made in the struggle between the German churches and the new Nazi government. Above all we see Bonhoeffer, with rare grace and warmth, finding ways gently to guide a strong-minded adolescent into a flourishing life and faith.

Though the other half of this correspondence, Ernst Cromwell's letters to Bonhoeffer, has been lost, Ernst is nonetheless a full partner in it. Bonhoeffer took to this precocious, intelligent and lively confirmand, still in his teens when the Berlin-educated pastor met him, and welcomed him into his confidence. After distance and time drew them apart, the course of Ernst Cromwell's life was eventful in its own

---

1 See, e.g., Keith Clements, *The SPCK Introduction to Bonhoeffer* (London: SPCK, 2010); Joel Lawrence, *Bonhoeffer: A Guide for the Perplexed* (London: T&T Clark, 2010) and Stephen Plant, *Bonhoeffer* (London: T&T Clark, 2004).

right. Distinct from and in addition to any interest these letters foster in Bonhoeffer, they ought also to stimulate interest in the lives of the many families who sought refuge in Britain from Nazi misrule, and whose welcome by some Britons was alloyed with deep suspicion by others, not least by the British government that interned so many of them indiscriminately after the fall of France in 1940.

The first section of what follows is an essay that fills out some of the background to the letters, setting them in context for any whose knowledge of the period is hazy. This 'introductory' essay also aims to amplify some of the key themes in the letters, including the development of Bonhoeffer's theology of life together in Christ, the practice of silence, the impact of the church struggle on friendship, and the central role played by Jesus' Sermon on the Mount, both in their author's thinking and in what Ernest Cromwell remembers of his preparation for confirmation. This is followed by the transcript of an interview with Ernest Cromwell in which some of the biographical background to the letters is spelled out. Then come the letters themselves with extensive footnotes making sense of details in the letters that would not be immediately apparent to most readers, as well as several comments on issues in their translation. Finally, Toni Burrowes-Cromwell uses her background in the area of international development and youth services to connect this historical relationship with some contemporary challenges – not least, linking faith with practice and how the Church engages in mentoring young people.

In spite of its relatively modest length, an unusually large number of people has contributed to the appearance of this short book. At the earliest stage Mike King, then leader of World Church Relationships at Methodist Church House in London, helped put Toni in touch with Stephen. Knut Hammerling and the Revd Burkhard Scheffler of the Bonhoeffer Haus in Berlin also supported the work. By January 2012, a small group of scholars and research students had met at Trinity Hall, Cambridge, to read the letters. The discussions that took place on that occasion have informed this volume and helped to shape many of the footnotes. Initial transcription of the letters was undertaken by Jelena Beljin. Included in the first group to see them were not only Professor Ralf K. Wüstenberg, Professor Clifford Green, Executive Director of the Dietrich Bonhoeffer Works, and Dr Keith Clements, who edited the London volume of Bonhoeffer's writings (DBWE 13), but also Ernest Cromwell's granddaughter, Eloise Cromwell, who helped bring the story 'off the page' as a living family history.

As an expert on Dietrich Bonhoeffer's handwriting (and on much else about him) Dr Ilse Tödt's subsequent assistance in accurately transcribing the text has been invaluable. The translation of the letters themselves is by Isabel Best, who, as translator of *Dietrich Bonhoeffer: London 1933–1935*, Volume 13 of the Dietrich Bonhoeffer Works in English, was familiar not only with the conventions of the Bonhoeffer translation project as a whole, but with this period in particular. Our thanks are given to Brother Steven CR, Archivist of the Community of the Resurrection, who kindly sent a copy of the minutes for the House Chapter that mention Bonhoeffer's visit.

The delegated responsibility for handling copyright issues on Bonhoeffer's literary legacy lies with Gütersloher Verlagshaus, while copyright on all English translations of Bonhoeffer is held by Augsburg/Fortress. We are grateful for the patient and generous way in which some complex copyright issues have been resolved, as well as, of course, for the permission to publish at all. Philip Law at SPCK immediately saw the potential for this volume, and is responsible for unravelling the rights issues.

By kind agreement with Gütersloher Verlagshaus and Fortress Press, this English edition is published by SPCK Publishing (UK) in 2013. The letters in their original German will be published in the *Dietrich Bonhoeffer Jahrbuch 6* by Gütersloher Verlagshaus, publishers of the *Dietrich Bonhoeffer Werke*, who oversee the rights to Bonhoeffer's literary estate. The English text of the letters and notes appear in the Dietrich Bonhoeffer Works English edition, copyright Fortress Press, Minneapolis. The letters from 8 June 1935 onward will appear in Volume 14, *Theological Education at Finkenwalde, 1935–1937*, scheduled for publication in the United States late in 2013; the letters prior to 8 June 1935 belong in DBWE 13, *London 1933–1935*, already published in 2007; they will be incorporated into future editions. We are grateful to all those whose agreement has made these arrangements possible, including Professor Clifford Green, Executive Director and Dr Victoria Barnett, the General Editor of the Dietrich Bonhoeffer Works; Philip Law, our commissioning editor at SPCK; the Gütersloher Verlagshaus and the Fortress Press.

We extend thanks also to Rowland Whitehead who provided encouragement from his Caribbean ministry base; Revd Dr Frank Goveia of the Rye Lane Chapel in London; Prof. David Lyon, Professor of Sociology at Queens University, Ontario, Canada; and Dr Keith White, Director of the Millgrove Residential Community for Children in London and the Child Theology Movement. These men are all radical thinkers and extraordinary ministers who gave tremendous support throughout this writing journey.

Our deepest thanks are owed to Ernest Cromwell for his foresight in keeping the letters published here and for his patience in sitting through many hours of personal interviews and conversations, in providing the initial working translation of the letters, and recalling further details from his teenage life. We hope that in our writing we have been guided by his sober admonition not to be such a one as '*hört das Gras wachsen*'.

# Abbreviations

| | |
|---|---|
| DBW 14 | *Dietrich Bonhoeffer: Illegale Theologenausbildung: Finkenwalde 1935–1937*, edited by O. Dudzus and J. Henkys (Munich: Chr. Kaiser Verlag, 1996) |
| DBWE 2 | Dietrich Bonhoeffer, *Act and Being*, English edition edited by Wayne Whitson Floyd (Minneapolis: Fortress Press, 1996) |
| DBWE 5 | Dietrich Bonhoeffer, *Life Together/Prayerbook of the Bible*, English edition edited by Geffrey B. Kelly (Minneapolis: Fortress Press, 1996) |
| DBWE 8 | Dietrich Bonhoeffer, *Letters and Papers from Prison*, English edition edited by John de Gruchy (Minneapolis: Fortress Press, 2010) |
| DBWE 11 | *Dietrich Bonhoeffer: Ecumenical, Academic and Pastoral Work: 1931–1932*, English edition edited by V. J. Barnett, M. Brocker and M. B. Lukens (Minneapolis: Fortress Press, 2012) |
| DBWE 12 | *Dietrich Bonhoeffer: Berlin: 1932–1933*, English edition edited by Larry L. Rasmussen (Minneapolis: Fortress Press, 2009) |
| DBWE 13 | *Dietrich Bonhoeffer: London, 1933–1935*, English edition edited by Keith Clements (Minneapolis: Fortress Press, 2007) |
| DB-ER | Eberhard Bethge, *Dietrich Bonhoeffer: A Biography*, revised edition (Minneapolis: Fortress Press, 2000) |
| KC | Keith Clements, *Bonhoeffer and Britain* (London: Churches Together in Britain and Ireland, 2006) |

# 1

# A friendship to be grateful for: Bonhoeffer's letters to Ernst Cromwell

That I got to know your father and mother and all of you has become very important to me, especially in these times. I really think of you as good friends, for whom one must forever be grateful.

(Dietrich Bonhoeffer to Ernst Cromwell, 27 March 1936)

*NB: On joining the British Army in 1941 Ernst Cromwell changed his name to Ernest Cromwell, which was not only permitted but also encouraged for members of the armed forces serving in combat zones in order to protect them in case of capture. In this chapter we therefore refer to Ernst when discussing him before 1941 and Ernest thereafter.*

## Bonhoeffer, confirmation and 'mentoring' the young

The friendship begins with a request that Bonhoeffer confirm Ernst Cromwell as a baptized member of the Christian Church. The importance for Lutherans of catechetical training for Christians has its origins with Martin Luther himself. In 1529 Luther published his *Large Catechism* intended as a manual for clergy in the practice of Christian initiation. Following a pastoral tour, in 1551 Luther published a second, *Small Catechism* in response to what he took to be widespread ignorance of doctrine among the 'common people' – and among the clergy who were supposed to teach them. Though Luther identifies the want of theological knowledge as the problem, in point of fact the *Small Catechism* is concerned at least as much with moral formation, recognizing, as does the Lord's Prayer, that the duty of Christians to God is in balance with their duty to their neighbours.

Given the importance of catechesis to Luther it is perhaps unsurprising that in 1931 Bonhoeffer and his friend Franz Hildebrandt wrote a catechism together titled 'As You Believe, So You Receive'[1] that tried to express simply 'what the Lutheran faith is saying today'. The catechism is carefully structured. Even here, however, a handwritten addition to his copy hints at the approach Bonhoeffer would take with Ernst: questions and answers challenge 'confirmands to independent reflection. The confirmand today needs someone to expect to make something of him'.[2]

The theological origins of the new catechism lay for Bonhoeffer in the dissertation he had written to qualify as a university lecturer. In the closing section of *Act and Being*, his demandingly technical study of revelation, Bonhoeffer considers what Christians can learn about their faith from the insight that children have their whole future ahead of them:

> Baptism is the call to the human being into childhood, a call that can be understood only eschatologically . . . Faith is able to fix upon baptism as the unbreakable Word of God, the eschatological foundation of its life . . .[3]

That Bonhoeffer had this 'problem' in mind as he approached the issue of the training of those who would, as young adults, confirm the promises made on their behalf at their infant baptism is suggested by the jokey inscription he wrote on the front cover of the complimentary copy of *Akt und Sein* that he gave to Hildebrandt: 'And will a catechism come now from this!?'[4]

---

1 See DBWE 11 2/7 pp. 258–67.

2 DBWE 11 2/7 note 4, p. 259.

3 DBWE 2 pp. 159–60.

4 In German: '*Und daraus soll nun ein Katechismus werden!? Ihr Dietrich Bonhoeffer*'; see DB-ER p. 186 where Bethge slightly misquotes the dedication. The original copy is now in the Bonhoeffer Archive at Union Seminary, New York.

There is no evidence of the extent to which Bonhoeffer put his jointly written catechism into practice when he was instructed to lead a confirmation class at Zionskirche in the Mitte district of Berlin[5] from November 1931 to March 1932, but it must surely have contributed to his approach. Bethge reports that the class was out of hand when Bonhoeffer took it over. The boys, 40 of them, threw things at him as he climbed the stairs to meet them and reacted to his name by chanting 'Bon, Bon, Bon!'[6] He dealt with this by quietly telling a story about his time in New York and the class became silent in order to hear him. He rented a room nearby and instructed the landlady to leave it unlocked so the boys could use it. He also rented nine acres of land on the Berlin outskirts with a wooden house to which he could take his class, and took a group of them on a walking tour of the Harz Mountains. Before the confirmation service itself, Bonhoeffer distributed cloth to make new clothes for those being confirmed. Richard Rother, one of those confirmed in this group, reports that Bonhoeffer took care to choose a Bible text to give to each of them for their confirmation.[7] Bonhoeffer's work on a catechism and his experience of preparing a large group for confirmation meant that when he came to prepare Ernst Cromwell for confirmation he had a wealth of theological and practical wisdom to draw on.

## How Bonhoeffer came to London

Bonhoeffer's decision to seek an appointment as a pastor to German-speaking Christians in London was by no means straightforward. In Germany in the twentieth century, and largely still now, individuals

---

5 Almost all the Bonhoeffer literature indicates that Zionskirche was in the Berlin district of Wedding, but to be precise the church was built in the Rosenthaler Vorstadt which was divided into Mitte, Prenzlauer Berg, and Wedding in 1920. Zionskirche sits almost exactly on the spot where Wedding, Prenzlauer Berg and Mitte meet, falling just in Mitte. In a series of boundary changes in 2001 Wedding was subsumed into Mitte.

6 DB-ER p. 226.

7 Richard Rother, 'A Confirmation Class in Wedding', in eds W.-D. Zimmermann and R. G. Smith, *I Knew Dietrich Bonhoeffer* (London: Fontana, 1973), p. 58.

who have studied theology must decide whether they want to serve in pastoral ministry or pursue an academic career. Already in 1935 Bonhoeffer felt torn between these two directions. He had qualified as a university lecturer in 1930, receiving his 'habilitation', the certificate needed to teach in the German university system, when he was only 24 years old. Members of his faculty in Berlin spoke of him as the most promising theologian of his generation. Yet Bonhoeffer had also enjoyed a year as an assistant minister in the German-speaking congregation in Barcelona and had made the most of some challenging pastoral work not only at Zionskirche but also, from October 1931 to 1933, as chaplain at the technical college at Berlin-Charlottenberg. Bonhoeffer's decision to take up a pastoral appointment in London did not altogether close off the possibility of a future career in the university, but it did put a brake on it and indicate the earnestness of his sense of calling to serve the Church.

The decision also had in it several more 'human' elements. Bonhoeffer loved travel: while a student in New York, for example, he took the trouble to travel both to Cuba and to Mexico. London, then as now one of the world's truly great cities, appealed. It also meant he would have his own house instead of squatting with his parents. Finally, Bonhoeffer and his distant cousin Elizabeth Zinn had, by mutual consent, ended the 'understanding' they had had about their relationship; this really was the perfect moment to try something new. For all these reasons a move to London looked like the perfect course to take. What made the decision to leave Germany vexing was what it could be taken to suggest about Bonhoeffer's participation in the German church struggle.

Following Adolf Hitler's appointment as Reich Chancellor in January 1933, the Nazi government moved swiftly to neutralize potential church opposition and to conform the churches, along with every other significant previously independent group, to Nazi organization and control. On 20 July 1933, the Nazi government signed a concordat (a treaty) with the Holy See that included provisions to disband the Catholic Centre Party, the only remaining effective political opposition to the Nazis. At the same time they began the process of imposing unity upon the Protestant *Landeskirchen* or regional churches. On paper, this might have looked like a reasonable thing to do: one nation, one Church. But the 32 regional churches in existence in 1933 each had long independent histories. Moreover, though Protestant, they did not all belong to the same confessional tradition: a majority was Lutheran, some were Reformed (i.e. Calvinist), and some were unions of both Lutheran and Reformed traditions. As early as 1931 pressure groups began to form to influence the political direction of the German Protestant churches. The *Deutsche Christen* (German Christians), a strongly nationalist group with anti-Semitic character-istics, welcomed Hitler and campaigned for one national Church. In opposition, a Pastors' Emergency League coalesced around Martin Niemöller, pastor of the suburban Dahlem parish church in Berlin. Bonhoeffer was one of the first to join and was one of the league's most indefatigable campaigners. The Pastors' Emergency League attracted a sizeable membership but quite quickly gave way to the *Bekennende Kirche*, the Confessing (or sometimes Confessional) Church.

The issues dividing these two church parties were more complex than might at first appear and two distinct sets of issues were inter-woven in their disputes. Certainly politics had something to do with it; yet by no means all *Deutsche Christen* were Nazis and by no means all members of the Confessing Church were anti-Nazi. Many who were committed nationalists opposed the formation of one *Reichskirche* on strictly theological grounds. To understand this, we need to recall the foundations of Lutheran political theology: according to Luther reli-gious leaders had their authority from God, but so did secular rulers. These two authorities were not intended by God to compete with, but to complement and even to support, each other. Key to the theo-logical health of this symbiotic relationship was that neither authority interfered in the divinely given authority of the other so long as it was doing its job properly. Luther conceived circumstances in which it was appropriate for the state to intervene in church life, and for the Church to intervene in secular matters *if* such intervention could be justified by a clear failure of the state to govern wisely in its 'realm' or of the Church to govern wisely in its. A Reformed political theology was not identical to a Lutheran, but was similar on many essential points. The question facing Protestant Christians in Germany from 1933 was therefore: 'Has the state exceeded its divine authority in the case of insisting upon a single national Church governed by a single *Reichsbischof*?'

To an extent Martin Niemöller embodied some of this complexity. A former U-boat commander, Niemöller was a committed German nationalist and, though not anti-Semitic, was instinctively sympathetic to many Nazi policies. Yet theologically he held strong views that the Nazi state should keep out of the affairs of the Church unless the Church had failed in the exercise of its duty. By contrast Bonhoeffer was *both* politically opposed to Nazism *and* theologically convinced that this particular intervention by the Nazi state was improper. To Bonhoeffer, Niemöller was certainly an ally, but he was also a 'starry-eyed idealist' because he thought he could outdo the National Socialists in nationalist fervour.[8]

In August 1933 Bonhoeffer, together with another Lutheran theologian, Hermann Sasse, was commissioned to draft a theological basis for the nascent Confessing Church; it was named the Bethel Confession after the place where they undertook the work. They drafted two versions that make bold theological statements concerning the Christian Church.[9] Though Bonhoeffer and Sasse's statements on Church/state relations were in keeping with Lutheran orthodoxy, in the context of the church struggle they proved explosive. After stating the Lutheran view that worldly government is ordained by God, they continued that '[t]he church can never be absorbed by worldly government, that is, it can never be "built into" the structure of a state. The content of its proclamation always places it over against all worldly authority'.[10] This ran directly counter to the policy of *Gleichschaltung*,

---

8    The phrasing is Bonhoeffer's: see DBWE 13 1/193 p. 135.

9    The Bethel Confession went through several drafts; the two published in DBWE 12 2/15 pp. 374–424 are the versions that Bonhoeffer worked on – and which therefore had his full support. After August 1933 he withdrew from the drafting process and he disapproved later revisions.

10    DBWE 12 2/15 p. 414.

the bringing into line or conformation of all aspects of German society to the Nazi Party.

Also included in the drafts submitted by Bonhoeffer and Sasse was a clause on 'The Church and the Jews'. From the perspective of Christian theology after the Holocaust/Shoah this section of the draft Bethel Confession contains disturbing elements; for example, it maintains the historic Christian claim that 'The place of the Old Testament people of the covenant has been taken not by another nation but rather by the Christian church, called out of, and within, all nations'.[11] Though intended to militate *against* Nazi claims that Germans were now God's chosen people, the assertion that the Church has superseded Israel as God's chosen people with hindsight theologically underwrote the anti-Jewish thinking it was intended to oppose. Yet the two theologians resisted firmly a racist approach to what was commonly called 'the Jewish problem':

> [t]he fellowship of those belonging to the church is determined not by blood, therefore, by race, but by the Holy Spirit and baptism . . . We object to the attempt to make the German Protestant church into a Reich church for Christians of the Aryan race.[12]

What even their draft failed to do was to advocate – as Bonhoeffer did later – that the Church must stand not only with baptized Jews, but also with non-baptized victims of Nazi injustice. When Confessing Church leaders got hold of the draft confessions they emasculated them by removing clauses likely to create controversy. Bonhoeffer's dismay at the evisceration of the Bethel Confession by church leaders keen to keep out of trouble is a major reason why he left Germany for London.

One leading figure in the Confessing Church movement who shared Bonhoeffer's anxiety about the Confessing Church's lack of courage was the theologian Karl Barth. From the time as a student

---

11  DBWE 12 2/15 p. 417.
12  DBWE 12 2/15 pp. 419–20.

he had read Barth's commentary on Paul's letter to the Romans, Bonhoeffer had respected Barth as a powerful and authentic new theological voice. Their first face-to-face meeting in 1931 did nothing to diminish Bonhoeffer's sense of Barth's importance. Though Bonhoeffer had engaged critically with Barth's theology, the younger theologian looked to the older as something of a mentor. Because of this Bonhoeffer did not write to tell Barth of his decision to go to London until after he had arrived, after which he waited anxiously for Barth's reply. When it finally came, Barth's response was friendly but uncompromising. Barth recognized that Bonhoeffer's move to London could be understood as a 'personally necessary interlude', but continued, 'I truly cannot do otherwise than call to you, "Get back to your post in Berlin straightaway!"' Summarizing Bonhoeffer's letter, Barth added, 'What is this about "going into the wilderness," "keeping quiet in the parish ministry," and so forth at a moment when you are needed in Germany?'[13] In this sharp criticism Barth was partly wrong and partly right. On the one hand Bonhoeffer continued to play a modest but useful role in the church struggle from London by mobilizing German-speaking Christians in Britain in support of the church opposition and by working behind the scenes to influence the views of leading English churchmen (alas, the gender-exclusive noun is accurate). And yet Barth did have a point: by absenting himself from the heart of the battle in what would prove to be the decisive years of the struggle, Bonhoeffer could be said to have been 'playing Elijah under the Juniper tree or Jonah under the gourd'.[14]

## How Ernst Cromwell came to London

Ernst Cromwell was born on 30 March 1921 in Nuremberg. His father, Philipp Cromwell, was a secularized German Jew who had served as a volunteer soldier in the First World War, first in Romania

13 DBWE 13 1/16 p. 39.
14 DBWE 13 1/16 p. 39.

and later on the western front where he was taken prisoner, spending time as a prisoner of war on the border between England and Scotland. Ernst's mother, Lotte Cromwell (née Rasch), had graduated in German from university. A convinced Lutheran Christian, like Bonhoeffer's own family and like many middle-class Germans she did not regularly attend a church, but she did have Ernst baptized as an infant. After the war Philipp practised as a lawyer and Ernst lived what he describes, in a memoir, as a 'very happy if undistinguished childhood'.[15]

Ernst went, a year early after some private tuition, to the Realgymnasium where relations between pupils and staff were cool but efficient and where the fact that his father was Jewish was not generally known. In 1930 Ernst 'acquired a little sister' (and later a brother) and by 1933, when Adolf Hitler was appointed Reich Chancellor, Philipp Cromwell's legal practice was thriving. Increasingly, however, the atmosphere 'became very unsettling and insecure'. The family domestic help was going out with a Nazi storm trooper who tried to persuade her to leave the family's employment. Rumours began to be repeated in hushed tones about friends who had been taken from their beds at dawn, maltreated and beaten. Judging that Germany was not a country where his family could have a secure future, Philipp attempted first to relocate to France, before moving to London to work as a clerk at a very modest salary in a firm making greeting cards. A short while later Philipp's family followed. Ernest recalls that his mother was impressed by the consideration of the immigration official who, seeing her with young children, called her to the front of the queue.

Upon his first sight of Britain, travelling from Dover to London Victoria, Ernst felt reborn. Not only was there the sensation of security after much uncertainty, but also, after the relatively joyless atmosphere of his German *Gymnasium*, he entered the 'fresh air' of the Beltane School. There, as he mentions in the interview published in

---

15  This section draws heavily on an unpublished autobiographical memoir written by Ernest Cromwell in March 1994; unattributed quotations are from the memoir.

Ernst Cromwell and his parents in Nuremberg, Germany, *c.* 1925

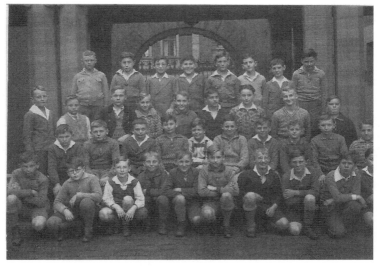

Ernst (bottom row, third from left) at Realgymnasium School,
Nuremberg, Germany, 1931

this book, an atheist deputy headmaster had an influence on his own
developing thoughts about religious belief and practice. Nonetheless,
the Cromwells were keen that Ernst be confirmed.

## Bonhoeffer, the Cromwells and the Sydenham church

It is unclear precisely when or how Bonhoeffer and the Cromwells
met. During his stay in London Bonhoeffer was active – with some
success – in finding financial support and support of other practical
kinds for a number of individuals and families who had left Germany
to evade Nazi oppression. Ernest Cromwell's memoir reports that, as
soon as could be managed after his emigration to London in 1934,
Philipp Cromwell qualified to practise law in England, specializing
in advising refugees on legal matters. It is quite likely that the two
men met in connection with one particular refugee or with a refugee family whose affairs Philipp Cromwell was involved with, perhaps

collaborating to facilitate a Jewish family's emigration. What is certain is that late in 1934 Mrs Cromwell fixed upon the German-speaking church at Sydenham as the right place and on Dietrich Bonhoeffer as the right person for Ernst's confirmation.

Bonhoeffer was on friendly terms with the whole family and not with Ernst alone. On 15 March 1935, Bonhoeffer wrote a letter of introduction to Baron Bruno Schröder of Schröder's Bank, which reads: '[t]he bearer of this letter is my friend Philip[16] Cromwell Esq., the solicitor whom I recently mentioned to you. I confirmed his son a few weeks ago and enjoy a very friendly relationship with the whole family'.[17] A short while later Bonhoeffer wrote to a member of staff at the bank, describing Philipp as 'a close friend of mine'.[18] The second letter in this volume dated 8 June 1935[19] is addressed 'Dear Cromwells', i.e. to the whole family (and, as we shall see, it is almost certain that the letter addressed 'My dear friend' of 3 March 1936 was sent to Philipp Cromwell). Taken together these few mentions of the Cromwells suggest a level of trust that had extended beyond mere acquaintance and shared interests.

Bonhoeffer's appointment in London was to two congregations.[20] In the East End of the city Bonhoeffer served St Paul's German Reformed Church. Socially, the congregation was made up of small shopkeepers and tradespeople, and average Sunday attendance was around 50. Bonhoeffer's other charge was St George's, Sydenham, which belonged (as formally did Bonhoeffer) to the United tradition which included both Lutheran and Reformed (i.e. Calvinist) confessional

---

16  The omission in the English translation of the third 'p' in Philipp Cromwell's name is a typographical error.

17  DBWE 13 1/208 p. 296.

18  DBWE 13 1/210 p. 297. Another recently discovered letter from Philipp Cromwell dated 31 March 1935, addressed to Bonhoeffer in Edinburgh, apparently 'crossed' with Bonhoeffer's letter to Baron Schröder's office (see DBWE 13 210a). Philipp Cromwell is aware that he is presuming on their friendship but the need to regularize his work permit is becoming urgent.

19  DBWE 14 1/4b.

20  The following paragraph is based on Keith Clements' *Bonhoeffer and Britain*; full bibliographical details are in the list of abbreviations as KC.

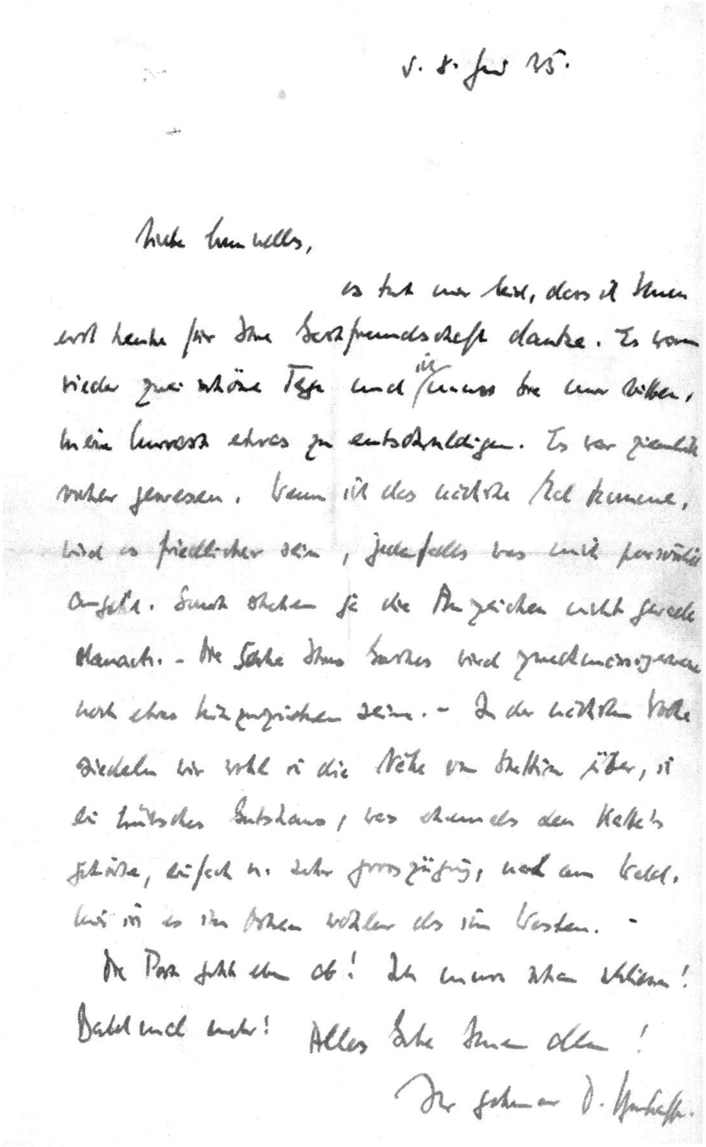
d. 8. Juni 35.

Liebe Cromwells,

es tut mir leid, dass ich Ihnen erst heute für Ihre Gastfreundschaft danke. Es waren wieder zwei schöne Tage und Sie müssen bei mir bitten, meine Unruhe etwas zu entschuldigen. Es war ziemlich viel gewesen. Wenn ich das nächste Mal komme, wird es friedlicher sein, jedenfalls was mich persönlich angeht. Sonst stehen ja die Anzeichen nicht gerade danach. – Die Sache Ihres Sohnes wird zweckmäßigerweise noch etwas hinzuziehen sein. – In der nächsten Woche siedeln wir wohl in die Nähe von Stettin über, in ein hübsches Gutshaus, [illegible] [illegible], [illegible] sehr großzügig, nahe am Wald. [illegible] es [illegible] [illegible] als im Westen. –

Die Post [illegible] [illegible]! [illegible] [illegible] [illegible] [illegible]! [illegible] [illegible]! Alles Gute Ihnen allen!

Ihr getreuer D. Bonhoeffer.

Letter to 'Dear Cromwells', 8 June 1935

traditions. The building in Dacres Road dated from 1875 and 'its members included diplomats, prosperous merchants and business people. Sunday attendance averaged 30–40'.[21] Bonhoeffer's manse was part of a substantial Victorian house at 23 Manor Mount, Forest Hill, a quarter of an hour's walk from the church. In this sprawling and damp building Bonhoeffer lived with his housekeeper and often one or more long-term guests, including for a time Franz Hildebrandt, his sometime collaborator in catechesis. Then as now, public transport between west London where the Cromwells had settled and Forest Hill was inconvenient, and the decision was made that Ernst should stay with Bonhoeffer in the manse during the Christmas holidays in the winter of 1934/5 to be prepared for confirmation.

## Bonhoeffer's 'classes' with Ernst

Among the most striking features of the way Bonhoeffer tackled preparing Ernst for confirmation is the extent to which it looks forward to his future interests more than it looks back to his former interests. Far from recycling the catechism he had written with Hildebrandt, Bonhoeffer appears, judging by Ernest Cromwell's recollections, to have rehearsed fresh thinking about what it means to follow Jesus that would later form the heart of his 1937 book *Discipleship*, perhaps the best known of all his writings. With Ernst, Bonhoeffer apparently showed little interest in talking through the creed, or discussing the sacraments, or indeed in reading other parts of the Bible. Rather, the classes seem to have consisted in what a contemporary scholar might call a 'close reading' of the Sermon on the Mount. Why did Bonhoeffer take this unusual approach?

We may get some way towards understanding what is going on here if we turn the clock back a year to April 1934 to Bonhoeffer's letter to his Swiss friend Erwin Sutz. Even before the Barmen Synod, which marked the high-tide mark for the church opposition, Bonhoeffer was clear that this kind of campaign would fail to deflect Nazism from its

---

21  KC p. 23.

course. '[W]hile I'm working with the church opposition with all my might', he wrote, 'it's perfectly clear to me that *this* opposition is only a very temporary transitional phase on the way to an opposition of a very different kind'.[22] It is worth pausing to register the extraordinary foresight such a statement required. In spite of his heavy investment in the newly minted Confessing Church, Bonhoeffer could already see that no amount of legal and 'merely' *doctrinal* witness would win through. Instead another kind of resistance would be needed, one characterized by compassion, by *suffering with* Nazism's victims, and shot through with the teachings contained in Jesus' Sermon on the Mount. 'I believe', Bonhoeffer wrote,

> that all of Christendom should be praying with us for the coming of resistance 'to the point of shedding blood'[23] and for the finding of people who can suffer it through. Simply suffering is what it will be about, not parries, blows, or thrusts such as may still be allowed and possible in preliminary battles; the real struggle that perhaps lies ahead must be one of simply suffering through in faith. Then, perhaps then God will acknowledge his church again with his word, but until then a great deal must be believed, and prayed, and suffered. You know, it is my belief – perhaps it will amaze you – that it is the *Sermon on the Mount* that has the deciding word on this whole affair.[24]

This 'amazing' belief that the Sermon on the Mount should have the deciding word in shaping Christian resistance explains why, in his 'classes' with Ernst, Bonhoeffer chose *this* biblical passage to be his main focus; it may also explain what he thought he was doing in his conversation with Ernst. He was, of course, preparing him for confirmation; but Bonhoeffer was also preparing his confirmand for discipleship of a particular kind at a particular moment: he was preparing him for the discipleship of resistance.

22  DBWE 13 1/93 p. 135.
23  The editors of DBWE 13 note that this is a reference to Hebrews 12.4: 'In your struggle against sin you have not yet resisted to the point of shedding your blood.'
24  DBWE 13 1/93 p. 135.

First page of letter of 26 or 27 March 1935, referring to a
'disrespectful letter' from Ernst

Bonhoeffer let the Bible itself do most of the work in his classes, which took the deceptively simple form of reading the New Testament and discussing it. As Ernest recalls, and as the letters confirm (note, for example, the good-humoured tone of the opening greeting in his letter of 26 or 27 March 1935: 'Thanks very much for your disrespectful letter . . .'), they were from the beginning unusually informal and open in their conversation. Whether this pedagogical method was carefully planned or fortuitously instinctive, in Ernst's case it worked: the Sermon on the Mount was firmly established as the cornerstone of his life. On 24 February 1935 Ernst was confirmed with two other members of the congregation. Bonhoeffer continued the tradition of carefully choosing a Bible verse as a kind of motto for each confirm- and, as Ernst recalls in his interview. Ernst's confirmation service was one of the last things Bonhoeffer did as the minister of the church: a fortnight later he preached his farewell sermon to his London congregation. But before he left Britain, Bonhoeffer had plans!

## The journey north

In March 1934 the newly elected German Christian church authorities took steps to neuter opposition to the new national Church. Among the steps taken was the closure of the seminaries of the Old Prussian Union – Bonhoeffer's own regional Church. To make matters worse, new regulations meant that any student now wanting to take the entry examinations to train for ministry needed to prove 'pure Aryan' ancestry. In response, the Confessing Church decided to open their own illegal seminaries and approached Bonhoeffer to take charge of one of them. This was in many ways an attractive proposition, but Bonhoeffer also wanted to travel to India; he had an open invitation to spend time at Gandhi's ashram, where he hoped to learn about non-violent resistance. In the event, after some months chewing the decision over, Bonhoeffer decided to return to Germany on condition he could leave off taking up his new post until the spring of 1935. This stipulation was because, in lieu of a visit to Gandhi's ashram, he had made arrangements to visit several religious communities in

England. From two of these Bonhoeffer wrote to Ernst, and his letters shed new light on the importance of these communities in shaping Bonhoeffer's thinking about life together in the Confessing Church seminary he would shortly be running. In spite of all that has been written about Bonhoeffer's work at Finkenwalde, the striking extent to which Mirfield and Kelham became templates is given surprisingly little attention.

Both Mirfield and Kelham owed their origin to the nineteenth-century development of Anglo-Catholicism and to the revival of new Anglican religious orders. It is to be remembered that training for Anglican ordination was a costly business and, in spite of trusts supporting ordinands, the cost of education prohibited candidates from poorer backgrounds. In traditional colleges education could also be highly academic with little by way of training for the realities of pastoral ministry. With many parishes in the cities and keen to extend their reach, Anglo-Catholics were perhaps more inclined to break the mould. 'Graduates' of these innovative institutions were, indeed, rather looked down on by those who had followed the more traditional route. To get a measure of the importance of Mirfield and Kelham we may note that, at the beginning of the twentieth century, the central fund supporting ordinands' training received 300 enquiries a year of whom only 45 would eventually be ordained. Kelham and Mirfield *each* received 300–400 enquiries annually but could only each accept 12.[25]

In 1892 Charles Gore, at that time Principal of Pusey House in Oxford, founded the Community of the Resurrection as a celibate community with a common rule and purse, dedicated to evangelism, and pastoral and educational ministry. Based eventually at Mirfield in West Yorkshire, the community had two elements that ran in parallel, a pattern that Bonhoeffer would very simply replicate at Finkenwalde. Mirfield consisted of a college training ordinands and, alongside it, giving consistency and a liturgical beating heart, a religious

---

25  See Roger Lloyd, *The Church of England 1900–1965* (London: SCM Press, 1966), p. 149.

community. These two bodies lived together, distinct but at the same time very closely integrated. The community took boys from the age of 16 – most of whom would never be able to follow the traditional route towards Anglican orders of studying in an Oxford or Cambridge college – and gave them a first-class education. From the latter, the former replenished itself. One catches the characteristic scent of Mirfield in a report of a meeting at which a member of the Community of the Resurrection met local villagers to explain the purpose of the community that had been founded in the big house nearby. The community was there, he said, to show that 'men can live happily together in fellowship and community under a rule. And sometimes . . . it takes a lot of doing'.[26] The House Chapter minutes for 19 October 1934 tell us that 'Pastor Bonhoeffer may come for two or three weeks in November or December'.[27] A second entry for 8 March 1935 reports that 'Leave was given for Pastor Bonhoeffer + a friend from Germany [i.e. Julius Rieger, Bonhoeffer's London colleague] to come for a visit at the end of March'. There is no evidence that Bonhoeffer did, in the event, visit in 1934 – the entry records an intention to visit and not the visit itself. The most likely explanation is that Bonhoeffer hoped to visit Mirfield in 1934 but that the visit was postponed until the following year.

The Society of the Sacred Mission, based at Kelham near Newark in Nottinghamshire from 1903, was, as its name suggests, founded primarily as a missionary order, but it too gathered to itself a theological college training clergy. Its founder, Father Herbert Kelly, had been a military cadet, and valued the ways organized training could enhance an individual's abilities. He also valued the self-deprecating humour of English schoolboys and recognized the importance of enjoying oneself. Kelly was still teaching at Kelham when Bonhoeffer and Rieger visited, and made a strong impression on them.[28] The buildings alone were impressive. Charles I had been held in the house

---

26  Lloyd, *Church of England*, p. 180.

27  I am grateful to the archivist of the Community of the Resurrection, Br Steven CR, for drawing this to my attention.

28  KC p. 85.

after his capture in 1647 by Scottish forces. The chapel was a later addition; dating from 1928, it had the second-largest concrete dome in England. As one member of the community joked in doggerel,

> We give our life
> We give our all
> Inside this great big tennis ball.

Abandoned for smaller buildings in 1973, the house is now the headquarters of the Newark and Sherwood District Council.

Previously it has been assumed – based on the fact that one lies further north than the other – that Bonhoeffer went first to Kelham and then to Mirfield.[29] The letters to Ernst make clear that, in fact, Bonhoeffer visited Mirfield first. A letter dated 13 March indicates that Bonhoeffer intended to leave London to 'visit various theological colleges Saturday next',[30] i.e. beginning on 16 March. On 20 March Bonhoeffer wrote the first of the letters in this volume to Ernst on the community's headed paper from Mirfield. At the end of the letter he asks Ernst to address his reply to the House of the Sacred Mission at Kelham from Monday, i.e. 25 March. Writing from Mirfield, Bonhoeffer makes light of the 'many hours of compulsory silence that I have observed during the last few weeks', a remark that, since he had only just arrived, must refer to something other than the practice of silence at Mirfield itself. Yet Bonhoeffer returns to silence a few sentences later to remark that 'the hours of silence here have come at just the right time for me. They are full of all sorts of thoughts and feelings that seem to pass by in a moment'. At first glance this comment seems to suggest no more than that Bonhoeffer is catching his breath after a busy period in preparation for the next phase of his life. For anyone familiar, however, with the role that would be played by silence in the seminary at Finkenwalde, Bonhoeffer's throw-away comment is pregnant with possibilities. The practice of silence at

---

29  See, e.g., the chronology in DBWE 13 p. 432.

30  DBWE 13 1/206 p. 295.

Mirfield was Bonhoeffer's first experience of silence in the context of a religious community, and it opened his mind to its great value. As Bonhoeffer would later write, reflecting on *Life Together* in Christian community,

> [j]ust as there are certain times in a Christian's day for speaking the Word . . . so the day also needs certain times of silence under the Word and silence that comes out of the Word . . . The Word comes not to the noise-makers but to those who are silent. The stillness of the temple is the sign of God's holy presence in the Word.[31]

Bonhoeffer adds in the letter that counter-intuitively it is in the shared practice of *silence* that one discovers one is not alone, but part of a community. It would be another four years before *Life Together* was published, but this key idea in it is already adumbrated in his letter to Ernst.

There was a very practical reason for Bonhoeffer's letters to Ernst during his visits to Mirfield and Kelham: they were co-ordinating their movements prior to meeting for a brief Scottish holiday. At some point Bonhoeffer had invited Ernst Cromwell and the others he had recently confirmed to go on a walking tour in the Grampians, a Scottish rerun of the trip to the Harz Mountains that he had made with his Zionskirche confirmands. In the event, only Ernst was able to go – apparently with financial assistance from Bonhoeffer as his note to Ernst of 26 or 27 March indicates. Bonhoeffer was in Edinburgh on 30 March and met there with Ernst. After travelling via Callander, Ernst recalls that in a shared room Bonhoeffer opted for the double bed while he was relegated to the single, from where he looked on with amusement when Bonhoeffer discovered his hot-water bottle had leaked. Together they climbed in the vicinity of Ben Nevis; photographs taken during the walk show that higher up a good deal of snow remained; the pictures also show that Bonhoeffer did not compromise on his sartorial elegance.

---

31  DBWE 5 p. 84.

Bonhoeffer on Ben Nevis, Scotland, March 1935

Ernst on Ben Nevis, Scotland, March 1935

## Bonhoeffer's return to Germany and his letters to London

Bonhoeffer returned to Germany on 15 April 1935, immediately following his Scottish tour. On 26 April he opened the seminary in Zingst, on the Baltic Sea coast (it would move to Finkenwalde in June). In May Bonhoeffer was back in London at the behest of the Confessing Church to liaise with George Bell, Bishop of Chichester, with whom he had become close during his London pastorate. For part of this brief visit Bonhoeffer stayed with the Cromwells. In his letter to Ernst of 8 June narrating his uncomfortable journey back to Germany,[32] Bonhoeffer reported on the 'more or less invigorating business with the authorities' that was quickly becoming 'part of [his] establishment'; the tone is characteristically light, but the comment hints at the tensions members of the seminary were already experiencing as a result of police interference. The letter to Ernst was evidently included in the envelope with a thank-you note bearing the same date to Philipp and Lotte Cromwell.

Bonhoeffer's subsequent letters were often sent to mark anniversaries, including the anniversary of Ernst's confirmation. Marking anniversaries is typically German, but it is also good pastoral practice. Bonhoeffer's continued concern for Ernst's Christian development is evident at several points. When speaking of the work of the Church he includes Ernst, as if he were himself a partner in it. In his letter of 25 October Bonhoeffer regrets that Ernst did not send notes on his Bible reading, as he had done in an earlier letter and as they had apparently agreed he would. In the same letter Bonhoeffer reassures Ernst and guides him, following an encounter with a conservative evangelical group of a very particular stamp, Frank Buchman's 'Oxford Group'. Bonhoeffer acts, in short, as a kind of unofficial 'spiritual director'.

Bonhoeffer also tried to keep in touch with Ernst's parents. In an undated letter probably written soon after 3 March 1936, addressed 'My dear friend', Bonhoeffer diplomatically returns half of a donation sent to him, presumably by Philipp, towards the cost of the seminary

---

32  DBWE 14 1/4a.

(Ernst remembers nothing about it and in any case would not have had the money). Bonhoeffer is presumably sensitive either to the cost in real terms of such a gift to the Cromwells at this time, or because he is reluctant to trade on their friendship. The letter dated 27 March 1936 is the last retained by Ernst and, we can be quite sure, also the last surviving that Bonhoeffer wrote to him.

To my mind, perhaps the most touching letter of the whole group is the last. As time passed since their trip to Scotland, as Ernst grew older and moved on, the letters became less frequent. By this stage in any case, as the start of the letter we date 20 November 1935 indicates, Bonhoeffer was himself distracted by pressing responsibilities. Perhaps Bonhoeffer even suspected his correspondence was being or might soon be monitored by the local police. Whatever the reason or combination of reasons, without any kind of falling out, the letter of 27 March 1936 has the feel of a temporary farewell. Its words are chosen with particular care; it is even typed, as if to give what is written greater permanence. He sees great change on the horizon for him. It is in this letter that Bonhoeffer remarks on the impact of the church struggle on his friendships. Some differences of opinion are possible between friends, but others are not. Bonhoeffer reports on making new friends, but also on losing others. 'The only concern is', he writes, 'to know, before night comes, who is a friend and who is not.' Such friendship has Jesus Christ at its centre: he it is who is the true basis of friendship because he is the Lord of truth and enemy of falsehood. In the group of people of whose friendship he *can* be certain, Bonhoeffer decisively includes Ernst and his family.

## What followed for Ernst Cromwell?

Following the excitement of the Scottish holiday, Ernst quickly settled back down to English life. Close to his sixteenth birthday an approach was made to Ernst's American relatives to ask if they would fund him to study at Lancing College, a fee-paying school with a strong Christian ethos and a reputation for academic excellence. They agreed, but after a year, upon discovery that this was a school rather than a

Ernst at Lancing College (back row, third from right),
Sussex, England, 1938

university college, they withdrew funds. Ernst's house master, with
whom he remained in touch until his death, without Ernst's knowledge invited a rich benefactor to tea to meet him as part of a successful
ruse to raise further funds.

Philipp Cromwell continued his legal work and, in a case that would
later slow up his release from internment, helped arrange what proved
to be (unknown to him) a polygamous marriage of convenience to
enable a Jewish woman to come to Britain. Following some canny
improvisation, Ernst's grandmother also managed to leave Germany
and moved in with the Cromwell family. On leaving school Ernst was
admitted to Keble College, Oxford, to read modern languages, but
after only a year, in 1940 war intervened.

Following the surrender of France and the pyrrhic victory of the
evacuation of the bulk of the British Expeditionary Force to Dunkirk,
the British government interned 'enemy' aliens. As Ernst comments
in his memoir, '[t]he irony of interning those who had more reason
to fight Hitler than most British people was grotesque'. After several

farcical experiences leading eventually to internment on the Isle of Man, Ernst was able to leave the camp by volunteering to serve in the British Army. It was at this time he Anglicized his name. He was assigned, with many other refugees, to the Pioneer Corps, where he was subsequently commissioned. The Pioneer Corps was unexciting, but military regulations did not permit him to transfer to another unit until, after supervising the burial of the dead on the Normandy beaches following the D-Day landings by Allied troops in 1944, he came under local military authority and was able to move into more interesting work that made use of his knowledge of the German language. From the summer of 1944 until his demobilization in September 1946 Ernest worked in a series of interesting positions in occupied Germany; at one point he was able to help some of his German relatives. After demobilization Ernest returned to Oxford University. Upon graduating he entered the legal profession in which he happily remained until retirement.

## Conclusion

Some of what we learn from these letters may seem of little importance to any but the most committed scholars. How does it alter our knowledge of Bonhoeffer's life and thought, for example, that these letters show him to have visited Mirfield before he visited Kelham, as was previously assumed? Yet even small details add texture to a life story, just as one life story can add texture to broader events in history as a whole. The letters in this slim volume bring to life a previously little-known friendship in Bonhoeffer's life. They show us Bonhoeffer as he tried to nurture the seeds of Christian faith in a young man in ways that would have a lasting impact on his life. Finally, to the discerning eye, somewhat hidden by the quotidian clutter of rail fares, jokey asides and banter, within these letters a few precious jewels can be seen sparkling when the light falls on them in a certain way.

*Stephen J. Plant*

# 2

# An interview with
# Ernest Cromwell

*What follows is a transcription from a sound recording of an interview conducted on 31 January 2011 at Ernest Cromwell's family home in Essex. This interview was transcribed by Nicola J. Wilkes. It appears here with a very small number of alterations that are there only to clarify grammar and syntax.*

STEPHEN PLANT: Well, thank you very much for making time to see me; I have been looking forward to meeting you.

ERNEST CROMWELL: It's quite interesting; I live very much on my own here with the family and I can't get out so any visitor from outside is welcome.

SP: Well, I hope we meet again. Can I just ask first of all what your date of birth is?

EC: March 1921, and I shall be 90 this year, this month actually.

SP: And what precise date? The reason I ask . . .

EC: Thirtieth of March.

SP: . . . is because in one letter Bonhoeffer mentions your birthday and it is an undated letter and I thought it might help me date the letter.

EC: Thirtieth of March. I think the letters are probably, if it is on my birthday then it will be the next year, 1934 [EC means 1936]; we came to England and I would have met him in '35 and I was probably confirmed in '35 and the visit we had in Scotland would have been in '35.

SP: What can you tell me about your parents?

EC: My father was a lawyer in Germany and when Hitler came he immediately saw the writing on the wall and started looking about leaving Germany because he said it wasn't a country where he wanted to bring up his children at that time. He tried France first and he didn't find anything that suited him and then he came to England and he met, or he went to clients of his when he was a lawyer in Germany, he did a lawsuit for them; [they were] called Raphael Tuck and Son who printed cards and that sort of thing and they gave him a little job in the office; they called him the foreign correspondent; I think he got about five pounds a week.

SP: He was of Jewish origin, is that correct?

EC: He was Jewish. His parents were Jewish and he was Jewish, but he was not practising.

SP: And whereabouts in Germany did you grow up?

EC: Nuremberg.

SP: Do you remember much about that period?

EC: Yes, it was my childhood; I was there until I was 13.

SP: Do you recall the tensions following Hitler's appointment as Reich Chancellor, or before?

EC: Well, when he, Hitler, came to power I was just a child and when Hitler came to power I felt, or it became obvious in the earlier part of 1933, that there were all sorts of tensions going on. When anything occurred my parents more or less spoke in whispers and didn't . . . I wasn't included in those conversations, but I heard about people that they knew – not necessarily Jewish, but some were Jewish – who were arrested for no reason and sent to concentration camps and one had to be rather careful of what one said. I myself was never troubled in any way. For one thing, because I was Protestant, I was in a class in my year where all the children were Protestant and there were no Jewish people in my class.

SP: Had you been baptized as an infant?

EC: Yes. My mother was . . . she didn't go to church but she was, you might say, Christian, yes.

SP: And you came to England in 1934 . . .

EC: In May 1934.

SP: . . . and you have already explained to me the reasons your father took that decision and the contacts he had in London at that time.

EC: Yes.

SP: What brought your family into contact with the [German-speaking] church at Sydenham?

EC: My mother was concerned about my religious education, not in the sense of formal religious education, but just about what sort of a person I might develop into and she must have contrived to meet Bonhoeffer when she knew he was in London. She asked me whether I wanted to be confirmed because she wanted me to be confirmed and I was a bit sort of indifferent about it. At that time I'd been through an agnostic phase actually, although my mother had always said evening prayers with me and I wasn't quite sort of . . . I was at a school where one of the vice-chiefs of the school was quite deliberately and quite openly with conviction an atheist and it rubbed off on me. Anyway I went along with it; it was kind of, you might say – hypocritical wasn't quite it – a less-than-open way in which I went along with it. And anyway, when I met Bonhoeffer I said yes. I wasn't anti . . . I wasn't definitely positively anti and I went along with it and that was it. I never raised the issue about belief or non-belief with him.

SP: Did he raise it with you?

EC: Well, he just assumed that I went along with his approach and I didn't disabuse him of it.

SP: You presumably attended some services at Sydenham?

31

EC: Yes, but that was only incidental to going to his confirmation instruction.

SP: Do you recall anything about the church and worship in it?

EC: Well, it was quite . . . it was not a high church; it was what you might call low church. It was all in German. It was for the German congregation. I think it probably started – I don't know the origins of it – but I suspect that there were German people in a sort of enclave or area there and that even at the First World War . . . they had a German pastor that ran the church and ran the congregation. And they had a house which belonged to the German community and which was available to the pastor and that was his home.

SP: Is that where you had your confirmation classes?

EC: Yes, I mean they were. I was the only pupil. It was direct teaching.

SP: What can you recall about the conversations? Did you meet regularly? What kind of things did you discuss in your confirmation classes?

EC: Well, I mean, when I was there it was during Christmas holidays before the actual confirmation because it was too far to travel [i.e. from EC's home in west London]. So I think it would probably be daily during the Christmas holidays and we would live together and we might have a little time in the morning which he called 'confirmation'.

SP: Can you recall what sort of things you discussed?

EC: Well, he would read a New Testament and that was it. He introduced me to the New Testament, you see, and that was it really. The New Testament did the trick for him.

SP: Was there any part of the New Testament in particular that he focused upon?

EC: Well, I don't know that he focused on anything on particular. I mean there were the miracles, the Sermon on the Mount and the sort of specific things rather than the story of the Passion you might say, but what I remember, you remember particular things and what impressed me particularly was the logic of – I am not very good at remembering these things verbatim – but the logic of what is generally thought to be unchristian about 'those who have shall receive' and that kind of thing. I don't think we discussed it, but I remember very clearly how the, what is generally thought to be, not religious in particular, how true that was, in fact, and, well, that sort of sums it up.

SP: Do you recall, how would you describe Bonhoeffer's manner in this period? How did he relate to you?

EC: Oh, he would just, we would just read the Bible.

SP: Do you recall meeting anybody in the house in that period?

EC: Well, his housekeeper, but I didn't have anything to do with that.

SP: But he didn't have other guests?

EC: Not really; he knew some people who lived up the road who were ex-German. I don't know whether the mother had died but it was a man with a son and a daughter who was slightly older than I was and . . . but that was it as far as I was concerned, as far as we were both concerned; it was more of a social meeting. I didn't meet anybody else that I particularly remember.

SP: Reading, Mr Cromwell, reading the letters . . .

EC: You can call me Ernest.

SP: Thank you. I am used to using the *Sie* form unless invited otherwise.

EC: Oh, I see.

SP: I am struck by in the letters that . . .

EC: That brings me to the point that from the moment 'go' he said, 'Call me *du*', and I called him that.

SP: Yes, the letters from the outset have a peer-to-peer quality.

EC: And as he sometimes . . . a bit impertinent but . . . from his reactions I felt occasionally, not at the time, but in retrospect, that he was a little bit surprised. He remarks on it in the letters a bit.

SP: It seems the content of the letters is really very friendly; as you say, you use the *du* form. It's . . .

EC: It is absolutely unique, so from the word 'go', and I was brought up, I was at an English school – I didn't have any of that formal German background in me.

SP: English schools could be quite formal.

EC: No, this wasn't actually an English school; it was a totally modern school that someone had started up privately [Dr Sheila Cromwell, Ernest Cromwell's wife, interjects, 'It was called the Beltane School – draw your own conclusions'], yes, a Beltane school. I told you about the vice principal and he was the vice principal I talked about and he ran a little private school in Berlin and he was an Aryan refugee when he left Germany and he paired up with an English man who was dead keen on starting a school and he helped the English chap to get it going because he brought with him a number of German refugee children.

SP: Do you recall anything about the confirmation service?

EC: No, except that he gave me a sort of, what you might call a motto or something about, something to do – I can't recall exact words but about those who are (I am not very good at quotations but I shall generalize – it is one of my faults to generalize what I think) or about 'the just shall find justice',[1] or something like that. I don't know whether he thought quite a long time about the right sort of motto to give me and my . . .

SP: It sounds as though it might be something . . .

EC: Well, it's partly to do, of course – my father was a lawyer and he might have detected the kind of, the way I would argue might be logical and . . .

SP: But it is also a scriptural . . .

EC: Yes.

SP: The practice of giving a motto at confirmation is common in that period, particularly by . . .

---

1   This probably refers to 1 John 3.7, which in the New Revised Standard Version is translated, 'Everyone who does what is right is righteous, just as he is righteous.'

EC: Yes, I mean he picked this out, you see.

SP: Tell me how your planned trip to Scotland came about.

EC: Well, he suggested it to my mother and she went along with it and because my parents couldn't afford it he paid for it all and so, what I have to do is to show . . . I think there is somewhere in the letter about, I think he also sent the money for the journey . . .

SP: In one short note, he sent you three pounds and six shillings, or something of that sort . . .

EC: The cost of the railway journey from London to Edinburgh and he met me there and we both stayed at a bed and breakfast or somewhere and he . . . the next day we went off by coach to Callander in Scotland, and the following day I had a walking trip up Ben Ledi which is the second-highest mountain in Scotland.

SP: At one point there was a possibility that some other members of the church might join you but that didn't happen.

EC: No, we were alone; the whole trip was alone.

SP: Can you remember anything else about that trip?

. . . [EC recalled the bed and breakfast hotel he and Bonhoeffer stayed in.]

EC: The reason why I remember it in particular is because afterwards I had to write an essay about my holidays at school.

SP: The period in which you took the trip to Edinburgh was the last period in which Bonhoeffer worked in London; he was already at that point preparing to return to . . .

EC: That's right, he was talking to me a lot of the time about his problem about deciding to go back or not. It very clearly was uppermost in his mind and it occupied his thoughts very deeply about whether he should or shouldn't . . .

SP: Did he consider staying in London and continuing his work there?

EC: Well, naturally staying in London was the alternative that he was

Ernst on walking holiday in Scotland, spring 1935

engaged on, but what he was wondering about was whether he should go back to it, go back to Germany.

SP: Was the reason he was considering alternatives because he understood that it was risky for him to return?

EC: Oh yes, he knew, he was very conscious of the fact that he would come into conflict, head to head, head on with the Nazi authorities.

SP: Did you discuss politics?

EC: He didn't discuss it, no, but he was very, in my present view, over-occupied in his mind with political events and every morning the first thing he did was to snatch *The Times* and look at the latest headlines and he read the leaders and so on which today I deprecate; I mean, I think it is all nonsense, yes.

SP: I notice in the letters that he assumes that the two of you are on the same wavelength with respect to political issues.

EC: Well, I was non-political; I was a schoolboy and I wasn't particularly interested in politics.

SP: Did you discuss his preparations for returning to seminary; did you learn anything about his thinking?

EC: No, I didn't know exactly what he was returning to but he was obviously returning to work in a church but he didn't go . . . we discussed, it might have been after he had been back and was already doing it to some extent but I knew what he was doing in Germany at either that time or by the time we were in Scotland; it would have been while we were in Scotland that we were talking about it.

SP: In one of the letters from 1936, a sum of money was sent as a donation to the costs of seminary, I think – does that ring any bells? [In fact the letter of 3 March 1936, to which this question refers, was probably written to Philipp Cromwell: see below – SP.]

EC: No.

SP: I think there is one letter in which he is sent something similar to five pounds which was a significant sum.

EC: I don't think so.

SP: He returned half the money.

EC: It might have been the change from the money – I don't know about this. I wouldn't have contributed to his costs over there.

SP: OK. Do you recall him discussing the possibility of his travel to India?

EC: Yes. My memory is at fault here because I thought in retrospect that he had been and actually met Gandhi.

SP: He meant to but didn't do in fact.

EC: I gathered that from what I read since, but . . .

SP: He was preparing . . .

EC: . . . I thought he had actually seen him.

SP: They corresponded; he had an introduction to Gandhi.

EC: Oh, I see. That I didn't remember. I remembered it as that he had told me that he had actually seen him.

SP: The letters that exist relate to that period in 1935 when you were preparing to go to Scotland and then there are a few letters from the period after Bonhoeffer had returned to Germany and you continued the correspondence through part of 1936. Did the correspondence continue thereafter or did you cease to correspond?

EC: I think it was really my neglect; he obviously, he always responded if you wrote to him but I didn't follow it up.

SP: In the way that one doesn't at that age, I guess.

EC: If you like, yes.

SP: But you kept the letters; they obviously meant something to you?

EC: Oh, I mean, it is a turning point in my life.

SP: Could you help unpack for me what you mean by a turning point? Why was it such an important relationship in your . . .

EC: Well, I think the real reason is that the meaning of the New Testament in my mind was established by that and the whole of my outlook on life and . . . what I observe and experience is coloured by, is based on that. I mean, I am not what you might call in a conventional sense a religious person but it was reinforced in me afterwards by . . . I went to school, Lancing College, and that is all based on a chapel and from then that is all I can say.

SP: Can you tell me how too the letters came to light after so many years? Did you recall keeping them or did they simply go astray and . . .

EC: Oh no, I don't keep things on the whole but I especially kept those just because I had them and they went in my loft with a lot of other things but not letters on the whole. There may be a few other letters but they were the significant letters in my life because not of what was in them but because who they came from.

SP: You, your own story, from the pieces I have been able to gather from Toni, is extremely interesting in itself. You were one of those, if I have understood this correctly, who were swept up and interned in the late 1930s, early 1940s, is that correct?

EC: Well, when France . . . the government panicked and interned everyone who had German in them and I was amongst those.

SP: And then you joined the British Army?

EC: And then I got the opportunity; there were several grounds for being released from internment and I said that I wanted to go into the army and I felt I had more reason to join the army than most British people and that's what happened and they in fact, they swallowed their pride and enlisted us from internment into the army.

SP: And you were in the Royal Engineers, is that correct?

EC: No, I was in what was called the Pioneer Corps and they were, in a sense, they were not engineers; they were the navvies. I was in there for a long time loading and unloading and doing that sort of navvy work and then I managed to get a commission and then I was, well, I was an officer in the Pioneer Corps and then eventually I transferred . . . the War Office were very reactionary

Ernest in the British Army at Cologne, Germany, 1946

or something and were not flexible . . . but once we got across the other side to France we didn't come under the War Office, we came under the command of the army itself and I got a job as an interpreter.

SP: And then you studied law, or well, you studied languages . . .

EC: No, I studied languages . . .

SP: . . . in Oxford?

EC: I had a year in Oxford in 1939 before I was interned and then I went back to it after the army.

SP: Which college?

EC: Keble.

SP: You were at Keble?

EC: Yes.

. . . [A discussion of Oxford colleges followed that is not relevant here.]

SP: You would presumably have become aware of Bonhoeffer's rising fame, I suppose, particularly from the 1960s onwards?

EC: Well, I knew what had happened to him, and . . .

SP: How did you learn of his death, of his murder?

EC: I don't know.

SP: You can't recall. What view did you take of the rise in Bonhoeffer's popularity? Did it seem strange, or otherwise?

EC: I wasn't as aware of the rise in his popularity as you might think, not until recently I think; Toni has a lot to do with it. What I thought afterwards is that from the point of view of Bonhoeffer's own outlook, it is hard to think of him fitting into the postwar world and that personally, I mean, my own outlook is a little bit more, you might say universal than individual and that one needs to look at the rise and fall of civilizations in a different way. I mean, I am not deprecating any component of his outlook – that was his life – but from the point of view of looking at the generality of things, life isn't like that. We are not martyrs unless we have to be martyrs; you have to live your own life. But it is a case of understanding what is happening in a larger way on the level of what happens if you looked at it from the point of view of 'God', if you like, for want of a better word. That this is what has happened is not something that you can change; it is just like how the cosmos works. That's why – I didn't mean to amplify this – but I was asked . . . I used to go in the barracks where we were stationed towards the end of the war, I went to the chapel on a regular basis and the padre asked me, 'Don't you want to become a padre yourself or take orders?' I said, 'No, it is the last thing I want; it's not the *last* thing, but it is not my life, because I don't see it in that way.' I couldn't commit myself is what I say. It doesn't mean to say I don't have my convictions about religion, if you like, but not in that way.

SP: Is there anything I should have asked you and haven't done?

EC: I can't think of anything except, I mean, you might ask from the point of view of Bonhoeffer, why didn't I do anything to get back to him. Perhaps it is not a question, but after the war when I was in Oxford I was introduced to Pusey House, you know, and the Principal of Pusey House, a fellow called the Reverend Hood [Canon Freddy Hood, Principal of Pusey House from 1934 to 1951] invited me and he was sort of angling for me to become one of their protégés and I didn't object, but he said – and he was one of those theologians which you might know more about them – that I should become a member of the Anglican Church and I thought, 'Well, if that is what they think, I don't mind', and he got me baptized again in the Anglican Church. Well, I had no objection. I mean, so what . . . but then there was a confirmation that he organized with some other bishop – I can't even remember the name of the other bishop – and there was a German congregation in Oxford itself and they all very kindly attended my confirmation and that was all right. It was a bit of a formality as far as I was concerned; I didn't need that. I don't know if there is something more that you wanted to know about me. Well, I think that is it. What I can ask you is, I don't know anything about all the theological side of Bonhoeffer's work, I mean it is not my line – is there something you can say about it?

SP: One of the reasons I asked you what you talked about in your confirmation lessons is because I was curious to see whether there were any connections between your conversations with him and his theological writings and it seems that there were some because he was very interested in engaging with Scripture in ways that was not simply about historical study. Academic theology in this period in the 1930s tended to be very historical and students were very rarely invited to make connections between the historical study of Scripture and issues of faith, personal conviction and practice. Something quite innovative that Bonhoeffer did in the 1930s with students was to try and help students engage with Scripture as Christians rather than just as students.

EC: And that was certainly borne out in my experience. And I don't think that he actually taught anything; he let the Scripture teach you and that's what it actually did. I mean, my insights into the meaning of what you find in the New Testament came from the Scriptures, not from him; he didn't tell me anything about justice or anything, but he let the Scripture teach me.

SP: And in particular in that period he was very interested in the Sermon on the Mount so I was struck that that was one of the . . .

EC: He also deprecated the religiosity that he would describe as Sermon on the Mount teaching that was all soft and cuddly and there wasn't anything . . . he deprecated that.

SP: And another strong theme that emerges, in addition to the Scripture, is his account of Christian belief that is focused on the person of Jesus Christ, so the study of Jesus Christ is very important in his theology: 'Who is Jesus Christ today?' For Bonhoeffer he seems to have been not simply a historical figure but a living figure.

EC: That only came out indirectly by what he said about and conveyed about the running of his *Bruderhaus*. [EC means here both the seminary and the religious community of graduates of the seminary that Bonhoeffer established alongside it – SP.] But he didn't teach anything about the person of Christ or his life, but he did convey to me a feeling that I wouldn't mind being a member of his *Bruderhaus*. I went along with that. But the thing is that I realized later, or maybe at the time, that I would feel that I would be sort of doing quite well in it; I didn't realize that the whole meaning of the thing would be to be the least amongst the brethren . . .

SP: That's very much, I think that is very interesting, because that does give some sense of the tenor of the *Bruderhaus* – yes, you are quite right.

EC: But you see, I was a young chap who wanted to be on the top.

SP: Do you think that there were any other letters which have gone astray other than those you've found?

EC: No, because I . . . well, there might have been, but I kept the letters that I had from him and I found those and I deliberately kept them; they went up in the loft with some other things.

SP: You know, there is one addressed to you that went missing that is in the public domain; it is published in one of his books, I think, if I can find it. This is one of the 16 volumes of the Dietrich Bonhoeffer Works, the German edition, and you are mentioned here in the index of people [see DBW 15 p. 700]; this is before anybody really did any research on you, but your father is also mentioned here.

EC: Well, he wrote to my parents of course.

SP: He did, and one of the letters is in this volume – is a very short note – and you and your father are both mentioned.

EC: [Looking at the index of names] Now, Cruesemann was a neighbour. I think he had children that I was introduced to but . . .

SP: I think Toni took a photocopy of this page; you can take a look at it at your leisure.

EC: There is nothing more on it, is there?

SP: No, but inside this volume [DBW 13 p. 285] there's a letter addressed to you but obviously never sent.

EC: Oh, I see . . .

SP: It looks to me like a partial letter. It is from Mirfield and there is a longer letter to you from Mirfield [i.e. in the letters to EC in this book]. It is on a picture postcard from Stratford-upon-Avon.

EC: That's right; he had a few days on retreat there.

SP: Yes, he travelled to several . . . he mentions another place he is going to visit near Newark; he visited several communities in that period to try and help him think about what he was going to be doing.

EC: Yes, I didn't realize until I heard what had happened to him that he had a very strong foreboding of his fate; he knew that it was a very, a life-and-death decision that he was taking, and I am not saying that he didn't have other thoughts on it but it was certainly one of the feelings that went through his mind, through his being.

SP: I am struck that he was thinking that through even in '35 and '36. In '39 he travelled to the United States shortly before the outbreak of war and the plan was to appoint him as a sort of chaplain to German refugees and . . .

EC: Yes, I read that.

SP: Well, he decided that that wasn't going to work for him, but his family were extremely well placed and his father was very well connected, a privy counsellor, so it is likely that he would have been very well able to assess the risk.

EC: I know, but even in 1935 or '6 he knew what was involved; I mean he hadn't crystallized his decisions then but it was . . . a decision that he would have to make at some stage.

. . .

EC: What I now started to recognize is that it is entirely my own fault; I could have kept in touch with him if I had written to him as a schoolboy or student but I didn't.

SP: My memory of being 16, 17, is that one just makes the most of the friendships that you have at that time and then you move on from them; it seems perfectly normal to me, not to have kept in touch.

EC: I am not suffering from the memory of neglect.

*The interview ends.*

# 3

# Dietrich Bonhoeffer's letters to Ernst Cromwell and the Cromwell family

Bonhoeffer's letters to Ernst Cromwell were all written in German. Only the last of the 12, the letter from Finkenwalde of 27 March 1936, was typewritten. The handwritten letters were initially transcribed by Jelena Beljin, assisted by Ralf Wüstenberg, and then thoroughly revised by Ilse Tödt, an expert in Bonhoeffer's difficult handwriting. The German manuscript was edited by Clifford Green, who also provided the first draft of notes; additional contributions to the notes came from Ernest Cromwell, Ilse Tödt, Victoria Barnett, Keith Clements, Stephen Plant and Toni Burrowes-Cromwell. No letters from Ernst Cromwell to Bonhoeffer have been found.

With the permission of Fortress Press we have incorporated virtually all of the notes that will be published with the Cromwell letters in the volumes of the Dietrich Bonhoeffer Works English edition; occasionally a note containing technical information for the scholarly edition has been omitted. Where all or any of an original note has been abbreviated for this edition, that is indicated by ellipses. Notes which have been added by the editors of this SPCK edition are identified by the author's initials and contained in square brackets [. . .]. Where Bonhoeffer himself puts the date at the beginning of a letter or where the editors have inserted a date or a probable date, this edition follows British usage. The symbol ¶, used in the Fortress edition to indicate the beginning of a new paragraph not in the original text, does not appear here. The Fortress edition also includes headings for each letter, which do not appear in this version. Where the original DBWE note number has changed for this edition, the original number is given in parentheses. We have retained the practice of beginning notes for each letter with '1'. For ease of reference we also include here the document number each letter will have in the volumes of the Dietrich Bonhoeffer Works English edition, e.g. for the first letter, DBWE 13 1/208a.

First page of letter from House of the Resurrection, Mirfield, England,
20 March 1935

[DBWE 13 1/208a]

20 March 1935[1]

Dear Ernst,

The many hours of compulsory silence that I have observed during the last few weeks have at least one good side. Now and then they provide enough quiet time to write a letter, and the pile of letters waiting to be answered gets visibly smaller. Today I will just send a brief greeting, but not tell you a great deal; I'll do that in Scotland. I hope you are back at work now.

Did your father tell you I received the news from Germany, at the last minute, that I have to be back there by April 15? This is now definite. In light of the most recent political decisions[3] over there, my heart sometimes stands still

---

1 Handwritten on both sides of two sheets; at the top of both sheets is the letterhead of the community: House of the Resurrection, Mirfield, Yorks. A handwritten addition under the date indicates that the letter was 'answered'. The Community of the Resurrection is an Anglican religious order in England that was founded in Oxford in 1892 by the Anglo-Catholic Charles Gore, and settled in Mirfield, Yorkshire, in 1898. Keith Clements reports that at the time Bonhoeffer visited, the superior was Father Edward Talbot and the most venerable member of the community was the retired bishop and former superior, Walter Howard Frere. 'At Mirfield it was the life of corporate prayer that touched Bonhoeffer most deeply; above all the way in which through the cycle of the daily offices in the course of each 24 hours the community prayed through the whole of Psalm 119' (KC pp. 85–6).

2 Germany had just regained the Saar after the plebiscite; many opponents of the regime had gone there for safety and were now arrested or went into exile; in early March the Reich made military service compulsory. On the church front, the Confessing Church established its provisional government in early 1935 and Gestapo pressures on the more radical elements of the Confessing Church were intensifying. The first mass arrest of Confessing Church pastors (700 were arrested briefly) was in early March 1935 after they read a protest statement from the pulpit.

when I think of what awaits us, but the needs of the Church are so urgent that there is no other way. The hours of silence here have come at just the right time for me. They are so full of all sorts of thoughts and feelings that they seem to pass by in a moment. The important thing, again and again, is not to become hardened and bitter or to worry unnecessarily, but to be able, time after time, to be immeasurably happy that there is such a great cause as Christianity, which can use the help of each of us in some way. And be happy that whatever comes, we are not alone; we are in fellowship.

In the next few days I must be sure and write to our circle of friends.[3] I've been going over in my head, day and night, what advice I should offer. It will be good, when I'm back over there, to be able soon to get our thoughts together on this. I've been thinking of you all a great deal in the past few days, and of you in particular. I wish the very best for all of you.

I'm leaving here on Saturday, for two days in York, from there on to one more monastery and then to Edinburgh. Say, do you think you could perhaps manage to leave by noon on Saturday, so as to be in Edinburgh by nine in the evening?[4] Three reasons: first, I shall have been in Edinburgh since

---

3   It is not clear to whom Bonhoeffer refers – whether these are the people in his London congregations who had refused, in January 1935, to recognize the Reich church authorities, or to his circle of closest friends like Niemöller in the German church situation. [A possible hint of what lay in Bonhoeffer's mind is given in his letter of 8 June 1935 (DBWE 14 1/4a) in which, remarking on his experience of 'the spirit of our community' 'where we are all of one mind', he adds that he counts Ernst 'as belonging to this group' – SP.]

4   In fact, apparently having celebrated the birthday at home with his family, Ernst arrived in Edinburgh on Sunday, according to the letter of his father to Bonhoeffer dated Sunday 31 March; Ernst apparently brought this with him since it begins '*Hiermit Ernst . . .*' (Ernst here brings . . . ). This is also confirmed by Bonhoeffer's letter below of 26 March.

Wednesday evening, and eager to be off on our walking tour. Second, I may have to be back in London a bit sooner than I planned (by the way, John and Inge[5] are *both* welcome to come; I've invited Inge too, but there still seem to be difficulties with timing). Third, I'd be happy to see a friend's face again, after these solitary days. But[6] do it only if it won't make *any* trouble for you at home, first of all; secondly, if you don't already have something planned for Saturday, and thirdly, if you want to.

My best regards to all your family, and especially to you.
Dietrich

[7]On *Monday*, please write to me at: House of the Sacred Mission, Kelham, Newark, Notts.[8] If I find no word from you there, I'll ring you on Wednesday or Thursday evening.

---

5    Note by Ernst Cromwell in the margin of his personal translation: 'John and Inge are teenagers of the German parish in Forest Hill.'

6    The following sentence and the closing were written in the left margin of the final page.

7    Written in the top margin of the final page.

8    Nottinghamshire.

[DBWE 13 209a]

[26 March 1935][1]

Dear Ernst,

Thanks very much for your disrespectful letter; I'm looking forward greatly to your even less respectful presence on Sunday.[2] I'll expect you on the train that arrives at (+)[3] in Edinburgh. Then we can look around the city a bit more and continue that the next morning; the rest we'll leave for afterwards, with the Cruesemanns.[4] I'd like to get up in the mountains as soon as possible, that is, by mid-day Monday.[5] By the way, I asked Mr Ullrich[6] to send a poncho for me to your address; please bring it with you. If *you* would like to have a windbreaker, just ring Mr Ullrich ; there's another one at my place. I have one here for myself.

If you don't hear any more from me, we'll keep to the time

---

1   Undated letter, handwritten on both sides, and in the margins of both pages, on notepaper with the letterhead: Society of the Sacred Mission, Kelham Theological College. Kelham is near . . . [Newark in Nottinghamshire – SP], which means that after Mirfield Bonhoeffer first travelled northwards to visit York for two days, and then turned south, arriving in Kelham on 26 March. The letter is obviously dated before Ernst Cromwell's birthday on Saturday 30 March. The Society of the Sacred Mission was the third Anglo-Catholic monastery Bonhoeffer visited. Founded by Father Herbert Kelly in 1893, the order originally intended to train missionaries for service in Korea. Housed in Kelham Hall since 1903, the order mainly trained priests for the Church of England until the hall closed in 1973 and the order moved to smaller premises. Bonhoeffer and Rieger were impressed by the lectures of Father Kelly and by the Old Testament scholar A. G. Herbert (KC p. 85).

2   In Edinburgh.

3   A circled cross, apparently referring to a time to be decided.

4   Gerhard Edward and Ingrid Elisabeth Cruesemann were confirmed by Bonhoeffer on Palm Sunday 1934.

5   This phrase inserted above the line.

6   Not identified.

as given above in any case! I don't know whether I should perhaps make a side trip to see Hahn[7] in Elgin[8] before Edinburgh. Then I wouldn't get to Edinburgh[9] until Saturday, and couldn't pick up your letter at the post office. If there is any change I shall ring you. However, I won't write to you again for your birthday,[10] I'll hold a speech for you in person, a day late. I[11] wish you all a nice day, enjoy yourselves, and I will think of you especially on Saturday. My greetings to all the family, wish your grandmother a good trip home for me, and convey my thanks to your parents for their letter, which I was happy to receive. All the best to you!

Warm regards,

Dietrich

---

7 Kurt Hahn (1886–1974) was an influential German educator who emphasized experiential education, founder of the Salem School in Germany, of Gordonstoun in Scotland, where he moved in 1933 following a brief imprisonment for his outspoken criticism of Nazi brutality, and of the Outward Bound organization. Brought up Jewish, he converted to Christianity in Scotland in the later 1930s. Hahn, like Gerhard Leibholz, was one of the German refugees in Britain to whom Bishop Bell turned for insight and advice. As of this publication it is not known whether Bonhoeffer actually visited Hahn, though he is mentioned as someone known to both of them. Hahn is also mentioned by Julie Bonhoeffer in her letter of 24 October 1935 (DBWE 14 107).

8 Elgin, where Hahn had established the Gordonstoun school in 1934, is about 170 miles north of Edinburgh.

9 From here to 'hold' ('I'll hold a speech for you . . .') is written in the margin of the second page.

10 Ernst Cromwell's birthday in 1935 fell on Saturday 30 March.

11 From here to 'convey my thanks' is written in the left margin of the first page, and the remainder above the opening of the letter.

Ernst on Scottish walking trip (sitting on a snowy Ben Nevis),
March 1935

[DBWE 13 209b]

[26 or 27 March 1935][1]

Dear Ernst,

Just a quick hello, to send in advance for your birthday (instead
of dragging the money with me to Scotland) your summer[2]
return ticket London–Edinburgh–London (3. 6/-).[3]

Get well soon!

Regards,

Dietrich

---

1  Handwritten letter, one sheet, undated, from Kelham, evidently before Ernst Cromwell's birthday on 30 March.

2  Inserted above the line.

3  Inserted above the line; Ernst Cromwell believes this was the cost of the rail ticket
to and from Edinburgh, i.e. £3. 6s. 0d., three pounds, six shillings, no pence.

[DBWE 14 1/4a]

8 June 1935[1]

Dear Ernst,

It's now been three weeks since my weekend[2] visit to you – and unfortunately you haven't repaid unkindness with kindness, but answered silence with silence – that's a pity.

When I arrived in Croydon on Monday, dead tired, there was neither a taxi nor a bus, so I had to walk to the airport.[3] I got there at 12:30 a.m. and just wanted to fall into bed, but was told everything was full and I would have to sleep in an easy chair[4] in the billiards-and-beer room. So the last I knew of London was the smell of spilt beer and cold smoke. The next morning at 11 a.m. I was back in Berlin. I was there two days for discussions, and then came on back to my people here.

Awaiting me here, besides a lot of work that had been left undone, was all sorts of more or less invigorating business with the authorities, whom we have recently come to know quite well and who, one might say, have become part of our establishment.[5] A remark I recently made on a Sunday about 'our brothers in the camps'[6] provoked a storm in a teacup and

---

1  Handwritten letter, two sheets written both sides. This and the following letter were written from Zingst, the first temporary location of the Finkenwalde seminary . . .

2  'Weekend' is one of several English words used by Bonhoeffer in this letter.

3  Combined from two smaller airports dating from the First World War, Croydon Aerodrome in south London opened in 1920 as the main London international airport serving Paris, Amsterdam and Rotterdam. Flights to Tempelhof in Berlin were added in 1923.

4  'Easy chair' in English in Bonhoeffer's original.

5  The ironic comment about 'more or less invigorating business' referred to his interrogation by local *Gau* officials.

6  Reference to the imprisonment of some Confessing pastors in concentration camps. See Bonhoeffer's sermon at Zingst on 2 June (DBWE 14 3/1), and the excerpt from

was apparently very salutary, and a lesson learned for us out here. The perceptive ones wanted to carry it out immediately but that was deterred, probably more by the economic interests of a resort town that depends upon visitors than by concerns about beliefs. Nevertheless, we could get away with that sort of thing again. Moreover, it's wonderful how it takes only *one* word, these days, to divide people's opinions,[7] winning over many, with fewer taking offence. Our community is holding together more firmly than ever. That too is something gained.

So you can imagine that I haven't had much time to write. I would have been happy to hear a word from you, but the three weeks weren't up yet! Meanwhile we are enjoying splendid summer weather, the sea and innumerable lilies-of-the-valley in the woods. We are working hard, but have declared four days' holiday as of today, since tomorrow is Pentecost. We are all looking forward to it. It's a very fine thing to celebrate these festival days in a community like this, where we are all of one mind. And you can understand that Pentecost has a special meaning for us. The Spirit of which it speaks is the spirit of our community; not an earth spirit from below, nor even the spirit of comradeship or friendship, but rather the spirit of brotherly love,[8] of obedience, of discipline and of unshakeable joy. Spirit from above, Holy Spirit, mercy – truth from above, righteousness, courage – that is what we pray for.[9] I have rarely

---

Gerhard Vibrans's letter, ed. note 1 of 3/1 [in which Vibrans describes Bonhoeffer's 'wonderful sermon' – SP]. Following the sermon Bonhoeffer was interrogated by the police because they had taken up an illegal collection for the Confessing Church; cf. DBWE 14 1/3.

7  Perhaps an allusion to 1 John 4.1. The German is '*die Geister sich scheiden*', literally 'to separate the spirits'.

8  See DBWE 5 27–47 on 'Community'.

9  See DBWE 5 38–47, on the distinction between a psychic (*psychische*) and a spiritual (*pneumatische*) community.

celebrated Pentecost with so much joy and hope. It is becoming more and more clear to me that everything will depend – in human terms – on forming such groups of people,[10] who cannot be destroyed by any means in the world, and who allow themselves to be led by this Spirit. From afar, I count you as belonging to this group, and we have already been experiencing, in the last few weeks, how one after another invited his friends to join us for a few days, and so the circle grows.

So you see that the work here is very satisfying and fulfilling, and indeed makes each of us happy, even though it often does not come without considerable renunciation[11] for a while. I believe and hope also that in this way we are performing a real service to the Church and to Germany – for how long, is not in our hands.

How are you? What are you up to these days, and what are all the others doing? My warmest greetings to all, and especially to you!

Write to me again sometime.

Yours as ever,

Dietrich Bonhoeffer.

---

10  At least from April 1932, Bonhoeffer had been talking about forming an intentional Christian community, focused on the Sermon on the Mount, with a group of his students as the core. See, for example, DBWE 11 434 [which is concerned with basing one's life on the word of Christ – SP], as well as his conversations in London with Hardy Arnold of the *Bruderhof* community (DBWE 13 114a pp. 158–60) [Hardy Arnold reports that Bonhoeffer intended to form a 'community of brothers with some of his students, based entirely on the Sermon on the Mount' – SP.]

11  On 'renunciation' see DBWE 4 101–3.

[DBWE 14 1/4b]

8 June 1935[1]

Dear Cromwells,

I am sorry that it has taken me until now to thank you for your hospitality. Again, it was a lovely two-day visit,[2] and I must ask you to forgive me for being a bit restless. The time just before had been rather hectic.[3] The next time I come will be more peaceful, at least for me personally. It's true that otherwise the signs do not point in that direction. It will be appropriate to keep the situation of your guest[4] under consideration for a while.

Next week we shall probably be moving from here, to a place near Stettin, an attractive manor that used to belong to the Kattes,[5] simple but on a grand scale, near the forest. I am more comfortable in the east than in the west.[6]

I must close, the post is just being collected!

I'll write again soon.

All best wishes to all of you!

Yours as ever,

D. Bonhoeffer

---

1 Handwritten on one side of one sheet; from Zingst. It appears that this letter, which is addressed to the extended Cromwell household, accompanied another one dated in the same way, which was addressed to Ernst.

2 Bonhoeffer refers to his short visit to London beginning on 18 May 1935.

3 A word like '*hektisch*' is implied but missing in the German original.

4 The reference is unclear.

5 See the editor's introduction to the German edition (DBW 14 7, ed. note 15).

6 At that time the eastern regions of Germany were more sparsely populated and rural. Although Stettin (today the Polish city of Szczecin) was a big port, its wider forested hinterland in Pomerania was very pleasant. Bonhoeffer enjoyed natural settings.

[DBWE 14 1/6a]

2 July 1935[1]

Dear Ernst,

I don't know how many weeks it has been since I last wrote. In any case it's been a long time, and since then I have received two letters from you, along with a few words from your mother, which I appreciated very much. The past few weeks have been entirely taken up with moving and getting our new house in order. We also fitted in a few days in Greifswald, where a united effort by all of us got the students and professors stirring a bit; they were sound asleep there![2] Despite [. . .][3] a few clashes, the overall result was quite satisfying, and during these days we ourselves also grew into much more of a community.

Then we managed to put the house here in order by ourselves, without outside help, and to equip it, for the time being, for our work. Farms in the countryside have been sending us all sorts of food supplies. We could have made good use of your help these days! Now we have a great cook, aged 78, and two unemployed 14 or 15-year-old boys to help her. That, at such low cost, is very nice. How would you like to have a job here?[4]

During this same time I had to do a lot of work on journal

---

1    Handwritten on both sides of one sheet.

2    See DBWE 14 1/24, esp. ed. notes 10 and 11. The German Christians controlled the theological faculty at Greifswald. Given its proximity to Finkenwalde, Bonhoeffer devoted much energy to supporting the theological students who were committed to the Confessing Church.

3    Word deleted, illegible.

4    Ernest Cromwell believes it unlikely that this invitation was ever seriously intended by Bonhoeffer. His Jewish ancestry would have made it imprudent in the extreme to work in an illegal seminary even in 1935.

articles,[5] and people tell me I have grown quite thin! Can you imagine that!

My summer plans aren't firmed up yet. What's certain is that I shall have to come to London at some point to break camp, but I don't know when or for how long. During that time I'll be less interested in making visits than in taking a breather, by which I mean playing tennis, swimming and reading. So perhaps I'll go to Torquay[6] or Cornwall[7] for 8 to 10 days. If I have enough money and you'd like to come along, I'll invite you – most likely it would be the last time for quite a while. It's really very kind of your mother to offer me special status as a guest in your home. But I think it's really time for some peace and quiet at your house.[8] I'll have plenty to do in Forest Hill during those few short days.

The rest of the holidays I want to use for further exploration of Pomerania, with a site for our plans for a House of Brethren in mind.[9] This is a real need. So I won't be able to go

---

5   See Bonhoeffer's article for *Evangelische Theologie* (August 1935, 245–62), 'Die Bekennende Kirche und die Ökumene', written between the end of June and the middle of July (DBWE 14 2/6, ed. note 1). At this time Bonhoeffer corresponded with Hodgson about whether he would attend the conference at Hindsgaul, Denmark, depending on whether there would be representatives of the *Reichskirche* present. The conference was a meeting of the Faith and Order Continuation Committee, which was to start preparing for the next World Conference on Faith and Order (Edinburgh 1937); see DBWE 14 1/6, 11, 12 and 14.

6   A popular summer seaside resort in Devon in the south-west of England, nicknamed the English Riviera.

7   The most south-western county of England, adjacent to Devon.

8   Ernest reports that the Cromwell family home in Wimbledon was a virtual 'open house' for visitors, a centre for friends and family and anyone who came from Germany. Each child had a room but was expected to double up to make room when space was needed.

9   See the subsequent memorandum written on 6 September 1935, and sent from Finkenwalde to the Council of the Church of the Old Prussian Union, DBWE 14 1/24.

to Montreux[10] for the conference. This will make my representative[11] that much happier.

The work here is going well. I think often of you all, and the congregations. But I cannot see coming back any more, the need here is too great. It's now just about a year since I first visited your family!

My very best regards to your parents, and to you

Yours as ever,

Dietrich

---

10 The Youth Conference of the World Alliance, 1–8 August, in Chamby-sur-Montreux (DBW 14, app. 1, p. 1044).

11 The ironic reference to his representative (*Vertreter*) is not to Martin Böckheler, pastor of the German Lutheran congregation in Hull, and later his successor in the London congregations, but to Bishop Heckel who attended and must have been delighted that Bonhoeffer was not there; cf. DB-ER p. 475.

[DBWE 14 1/15a]

[After 27 July 1935][1]

Dear Ernst,

This will just be a brief hello. Thank you for your letter. There is a great deal to do here and I don't have time to write. My plans for August have changed; I'm probably only coming from 4–18. VIII,[2] and with scarcely any time to travel because I have so much work. So, if you have other possible plans, as you say in your letter, don't make them dependent on my coming. I am sorry, but there's no other way. I do hope to see you though. Please give my regards to your parents and everyone in your house!

Yours in haste,

Dietrich

---

1  Handwritten, written one side of one sheet, undated. Written in July 1935, prior to Bonhoeffer's visit to London in August; see [below] 1/20a. In his letter of 27 July to Susanne and Walter Dress (1/15), he proposes holidays beginning 2 August [thus, the later date of 4 August mentioned here suggests he is writing after 27 July – SP].

2  In fact the visit was from 3 August to 12 August (DBW 14 1044). The 'VIII' is written above the line.

[DBWE 14 1/20a]

[13 August 1935]

London & North Eastern Railway[1]
Continental Services via Harwich
RMS 'Prague'[2]

Dear Ernst,

It was a terrible crossing last night – 'the worst we could possibly have', my steward[3] said. Nevertheless, the unheard-of did happen. The decision I took yesterday not to get seasick was a success, with the help of a whisky and of course fatigue, and despite the most awful noise from the neighbouring cabins. I got up this morning very proud, and seem to have earned the respect of my steward! – Now the train is about to leave!

All my best wishes to you, and to everyone

Yours as ever,

Dietrich

---

1  Letter, handwritten, on both sides of small notepaper of the London & North Eastern Railway, with a picture of the *Prague* above the printed letterhead. Above this line the name 'Ernst Cromwell' has been added with a stamp.

2  The *Prague*, built in 1930, was one of many owned by the railway company and served the Harwich–Hook of Holland route. Below this line is a stamped date, '10. Aug. 1935', added presumably by Ernst Cromwell. This date does not comport with the information of DBW 14 1044, that Bonhoeffer's trip to London was from 3 August to 12 August, and that he preached his farewell sermons on two Sundays, at St Paul's on 4 August and at Sydenham on 11 August. On Monday 12 August, Bonhoeffer wrote a farewell letter to Baron Schröder (DBWE 14 1/20), and this suggests that he took the train from London later that day and the overnight ship from Harwich that night, writing his note on the ship's stationery the following morning, Tuesday 13 August, before boarding the train. (Bethge's reference to a farewell sermon on 10 March 1935 (DB-ER p. 416) is to the beginning of Bonhoeffer's six-month leave of absence from the London congregations.)

3  In the original Bonhoeffer writes 'Stewart', apparently a Germanization of 'steward', the English name for a cabin attendant on a ship.

[DBWE 14 1/32a]

[25 October 1935][1]

Dear Ernst,

Many thanks for your letter. It's a pity you didn't send me your daily notes[2] as you did last time. But do as you like about that. I'm always glad to hear from you.

I find it rather unnecessary for Mr Goldschmidt[3] to be pressing his cause on you, more or less. But I think you can

---

1  Handwritten on both sides of one sheet. Undated by Bonhoeffer, but written in another hand at the top of page one is '25/10/35'; this date may not be exact, see [notes on dating in the previous letter – SP] . . . Written from Finkenwalde in the interval between the first and second course.

2  The 'daily notes' were notes on daily Bible readings that Bonhoeffer had encouraged Ernst to keep, and which he had sent in a previous letter.

3  Mr Goldschmidt was a (non-Jewish) German refugee who was at that time a teacher at the Beltane private school, which Ernst attended during his early years in the UK (1934–7). Note in the margin of Ernest Cromwell's translation of this letter: 'Mr G. was an active member of the so-called "Oxford Groups" not to be confused with the Oxford Movement of the time of Cardinal Newman.' Nor is it connected in any way with the 1937 ecumenical Oxford Conference on 'Church, Community and State'. The Oxford Group, started by Frank Buchman in England in 1921, was an evangelizing moral and social movement that in 1939 reorganized in Washington, DC, under the name Moral Rearmament (after 1945, it was called the Caux movement). Staffed mainly by volunteers, and active in a number of countries, the movement was still active and influential into the twenty-first century, changing its name to Initiatives of Change in 2001. In the 1930s it targeted recruits in Oxford and Cambridge Universities and in English private schools; Ernst Cromwell was therefore a typical candidate. Bonhoeffer had good reason to be suspicious of Buchman because of his invitation to Joachim Hossenfelder, the co-founder and Reich leader of the German Christians, to attend a London meeting of the Oxford Group; see Bonhoeffer's report of the visit to Professor Siegmund-Schultze, DBWE 13 32. See also Buchman's praise of Adolf Hitler at the 1936 Olympics (DB-ER p. 538), as well as Bonhoeffer's comments about the Oxford Group movement in his prison letter of 8 June 1944 (DBWE 8 430, ed. note 33).

stand up to him. I don't have much sympathy, either, for the public character of the group movement.[4] You say that the apostle Paul preached in the street – only twice that I know of, otherwise always in synagogues. And when he did preach in the street, he never spoke about his own experiences, what he had learnt, or even about his conversion, but rather quite objectively about the Old Testament and its fulfilment in Christ. The confession of one's sins, or of one's own sanctification and devoutness, truly belongs – say I, contrary to what the group[5] says – not in the marketplace, but rather in the privacy of your own room.[6] It's never good to talk too much about your own experiences; it's destructive of what you are doing. So I think your reaction was just the right one, and if you don't immediately know a right answer to something, don't give up right away. Arguments don't help very much, and especially not the ability to produce them quickly.

How are you doing otherwise? Write again and tell me more. You know, when I sometimes don't write for a long time, it only means that I'm extremely busy, and that I'm *twice* as happy when I get a letter from you!

Our work here continues, and until now without essential compromises. But of course there is a great deal of struggle. Recently I've been making myself pretty unpopular over the issue of the Jews [*Judensache*],[7] but with success as well. That's

---

4  In original 'group movement' written in English. See references in this volume and also in DBWE 4, 6 and 8.

5  i.e. the Oxford Group.

6  See Matthew 6.6 in the Luther Bible, from which Bonhoeffer's original quotes '*Kämmerlein*' ('chamber' in the King James Version). See DBWE 4 152–5 [on 'The Hiddenness of Prayer' – SP].

7  The reference is probably to Bonhoeffer's 1935 Bible study on King David (DBW 14 878–904 3/7), which became the subject of an attack in the Stuttgart Nazi newspaper *Durchbruch*; see DB-ER p. 526 and DBW 14 3/7 note 97.

the main thing. We are glad of every day that we can keep on working here as we are now. That could change to quite different circumstances. But even this doesn't frighten us unduly.

So, Godspeed – and greetings to your family.[8]

Warmest good wishes to you

Yours as ever,

Dietrich

---

8    Ernst lived with his parents Philipp (1893–1976) and Lotte Cromwell (1894–1983) and his two siblings, his sister Luise (b. 1925) and his brother Thomas (1930–95).

[DBWE 14 1/40a]

[20 November 1935][1]

Dear Ernst,

In the midst of my work, here's at least a brief hello. Today is Repentance Day, and I have just held the first Communion service with the second seminar session and the House of Brethren. This has occupied me greatly for several days – not least because of many conversations I needed to have with a number of the brothers. The House of Brethren work is now in full swing and our people are responding to considerable needs. One of the brothers[2] preached a sermon today, and tomorrow I am expecting the visitor we now know well[3] to discuss it. But this sermon was indeed necessary.

We are under the impression that[4] the path we are taking is soon going to lead us into serious disputes.[5] This is not so

---

1 Handwritten, two sides of one sheet, undated. 20 November was the date of *Bußtag*, the Day of Repentance. *Bußtag* was a Protestant church festival, observed as a public holiday in Prussia since 1893, on the Wednesday before the last Sunday in the church year, therefore eleven days before the first Sunday in Advent.

2 Ilse Tödt suggests perhaps Winfried Maechler.

3 Bonhoeffer probably means a visit by the Gestapo because the sermon was given by an illegal preacher.

4 A word that followed is crossed out and is now illegible.

5 The dissent within the Confessing Church itself was intensifying about how far one could compromise with the German Christians. Bonhoeffer's draft essay, 'From Barmen to Oeynhausen', written shortly after this letter, in January 1936, called for a clear stand on behalf of the more radical 'Dahlemites' [i.e. the group that stood by the line taken by Martin Niemöller and the regulations of the second Confessing Church Synod held at Dahlem in October 1934 – SP]. Cf. DBWE 14 2/14.

hard as long as we are together here, but at some point we shall leave here to live separately, each standing on his own. Then will come the time of waiting it out, of seeing it through, which already strikes fear into every heart. But it is only happening episodically so far, and the main thing is not to regard one's own importance too highly, to feel as though one has to be something like the sole saviour of the Church or of Christianity. That would be ridiculous.[6] 'Don't take yourself too seriously'[7] – even in these really serious matters, and especially in them.

How are you all getting along? I look forward very much to hearing from you. It's such a shame that I myself never get time to write – too much going on. By the way, I've started lecturing again at the University of Berlin,[8] and instead of all the other possibilities, I'm beginning with a scriptural theme.[9] That is more appropriate for a course of theological lectures. We'll see how long I'll be able to carry on. I'm in good health and have to be thankful for every day in which I can continue to work.

I think of you all a great deal, and often. I was very glad to have your father's letter![10] As always, my good wishes go out to you in all things, and peace and joy – and I'm sorry

---

6 A word that followed is crossed out, now illegible.

7 Bonhoeffer uses a common English admonition.

8 Bonhoeffer began his university lecture course 'Discipleship' on 12 November 1935; sections of these were subsequently published in *Discipleship* (cf. DBWE 4 65–182).

9 See the scriptural quotations at the beginning of most sections of Part I of *Discipleship* (DBWE 4).

10 [This is – SP] neither the letter of Sunday 31 March 1935 (cf. Meyer & Bethge, *Nachlass Dietrich Bonhoeffer*, 136; forthcoming in *Dietrich Bonhoeffer Jahrbuch 6* and in the electronic edition as DBWE 13 208a), nor the letter of 3 March 1936 (see below).

I can no longer do anything personally to further them. I think often of you in particular. Don't forget the time of your confirmation.

As ever, warm greetings to you all

Yours,

Dietrich

[DBWE 14 1/57a]

[After 3 March 1936][1]

My dear friend,[2]

Many thanks for your contribution,[3] which I have received. I was invited here,[4] with the whole seminary, for a study trip. We have been enjoying it very much, and since the archbishop[5] invited me to call on him, and the royal house[6] here has also been present on some occasions, we are very well provided for.

We'll have to see how it goes when we get back.[7] We're certainly breaking the law of December 2[8] every day, but so far nothing has been happening to us. Perhaps it will be different once the Olympics are over.[9] Otherwise, everything is fine. I often think of you all, though I don't have much time to write. We have a lot going on here.

---

1 Handwritten letter, one sheet, written on both sides, undated; date proposed by Ilse Tödt, allowing for time in Copenhagen.

2 The recipient was surely Philipp Cromwell, the father of Ernst, which would explain how the letter came into the son's possession. By avoiding a name Bonhoeffer is protecting strategic details. This is the only letter in the group that is not addressed to an individual or family.

3 A financial donation; see the end of the letter about returning money.

4 Bonhoeffer's trip with his Finkenwalde students to Denmark and Sweden was from 29 February to 10 March 1936.

5 A reference to Erling Eidem [(1880–1972), Lutheran Archbishop of Uppsala from 1931 to 1950 – SP].

6 Prince Oskar Bernadotte, the brother of the king.

7 That is, to Germany.

8 The law of 2 December 1935 was the Fifth Decree for Implementing the Law for Protecting the German Evangelical Church (DBW 14 1045); see DB-ER pp. 495–8. This order prohibited the Confessing Church from taking collections and holding theological and ordination examinations.

9 The Berlin Summer Olympic Games were held from 1 to 16 August 1936.

By the way, I just received a notice from the Ministry of Culture that, under present circumstances, I am no longer allowed to lecture.[10] But I am not at all certain what the final vote will be.[11] If major terror tactics are not employed, perhaps in the end we shall find ourselves better off than we expect.

Please give my regards to Seidler,[12] and ask him to remember me also to the others.

*If at some point I should need money again, I shall simply write 'the address you asked for is . . .' That means I am requesting £5.*[13]

Today I am returning £2 1/2![14]


In haste, warm regards

Yours as ever,

Dietrich Bonhoeffer


---

10 See DBWE 14 1/37, pp. 96–7.

11 This refers to the Reichstag vote of 29 March 1936, in which 99% supported Hitler's policies (DBW 14 1046).

12 Ernest recalls that Seidler was a Jewish refugee (baptized as a Christian) who lived in London. He was a former left-wing politician who was 'persona non grata' in Germany at that time. Ernest Cromwell believes that he assissted his father at a time of crisis in 1939 when Philipp Cromwell needed to get his mother Emilie out of Germany. As a result of Seidler's help, Emilie Cromwell was able to safely flee Germany on a Dutch passport.

13 In 2013 currency, approximately 300 pounds sterling, or 450 US dollars. This is the end of writing on the first page. Ernest suggests that Bonhoeffer's proposing an 'address' to which the funds could be sent is probably a coded message, which his father Philipp would have understood. This sentence is underlined in the original.

14 This sentence and the rest of the letter including the signature are written on the back of the page. Two pounds and ten shillings could be mailed in paper 'notes' (English) or 'bills' (American).

[DBWE 14 69a]

27 March 1936[1]

Dear Ernst,

It's now been nearly a year since we met and had our time together.[2] First I want to thank you sincerely for thinking of me, all of you, when confirmation time came round again. That made me very happy. When I think of that today, it all seems so very distant already. The past year has brought so much, at both personal and professional levels, both gratifying and difficult; it seemed so often that I had come to the end of the road, but then again and again things kept moving forward. Every day has been full of tensions and decisions, so that I can hardly imagine being back in our quiet days in London. Yet I think of that time with great affection, and of all that I discovered and learnt there, and especially of the people I met. That I got to know your father and mother and all of you has become very important to me, especially in these times. I really think of you as good friends, for whom one must forever be grateful.

You know, of course, that over here people are losing many of their friends, often in the most shocking ways, but

---

1  Two pages, typewritten on both sides of one sheet, with handwritten signature. This is the only typewritten letter in the collection. This presumably reflects the importance Bonhoeffer attributed to it because of its connection to the first anniversary of Ernst Cromwell's confirmation in London on 24 February 1935. [It may also have been typed in order that Bonhoeffer could retain a carbon copy of it; some of the phrasing in it seems more 'polished' than earlier more informal letters – SP.] The letter's valedictory tone may be indicative of increasing uncertainty resulting from the deteriorating church–political situation.

2  Reference to their time in Edinburgh and hiking in Scotland the previous year.

certainly also finding new friendships.[3] In the past year I have lost many people who were important in my life, but in the struggle of the churches I have also found a community again, one which is unbreakable from a human viewpoint. Its shape is becoming ever clearer, even now. The only concern is to know, before night comes, who is a friend and who is not. In this regard, it's good to know that over there in London are people of whom one can be certain, which side they are on. I can tell you one thing: more important than any insight, than anything to do with your fundamental beliefs, is to have people in your life with whom you know that you share convictions.

Now, as far as we can see, during the next year your life will not change outwardly in any essential way. Ours here will probably change considerably. What is crucial for you, in these quiet years that are still given to you, is to find and acquire the powers and the energy that you will need some day, in different times. And again, the most important thing is to hold fast to the truth, and not to let anything else influence you. But there is no truth without love. Hate turns truth into falsehood. Falsehood turns love into hate. This we know from the One who, in the midst of a world of terrible manipulation into falsehood and injustice and denial of mercy, has promised that he would be with us – Jesus Christ, whom we confess. Everyone here faces, again and again, moments of being hard pressed to give in, thinking, I can't bear any more of this standing all alone. Then it is very liberating to think that in his life and death, Christ

---

3   By this time the church struggle had bitterly divided pastors and congregations throughout the country, and even Finkenwalde had lost some of its students to the legal church.

became the Lord who has overcome falsehood, and that we are to share in his victory.

I haven't heard from you personally in a long time. But I think you still understand what I am saying.

Godspeed. Good health in this new year. And above all, don't forget the few things in life that are really important and that make life worth living.[4]

My warmest good wishes to your family, and to you.

Yours as ever

Dietrich

---

4    Bonhoeffer writes in English 'worthwhile living'.

den 27. 3. 1936.

Lieber Ernst!

Jetzt jährt sich die Zeit unsers Zusammentreffens und
Zusammenseins. Zunächst hab sehr herzlichen Dank, dass Ihr/ in den Tagen der
Konfirmation an mich gedacht habt. Das hat mich sehr gefreut. Wenn ich heute zurückdenke, liegt das alles schon so fern. Es war so viel im letzten
Jahr, berufliches und persönliches, erfreuliches und schweres, es schien
so oft alles zu Ende zu sein, und es ist immer wieder weitergegangen, es
war jeder Tag so voll von Spannungen und Entscheidungen, dass ich mich in
unsere ruhige Londoner Zeit kaummehr zurückversetzen kann. Und doch hänge
ich sehr an ihr, und an allem, was sie an Erfahrungen und Erkenntnissen
gebracht hat, und vor allem an den Menschen, denen ich begegnet bin.
Dass ich Deinen Vater, Deine Mutter und Euch alle kennen gelernt habe, ist
mit etwas ganz wichtiges geworden, gerade in dieser Zeit. Ich empfinde
diese Beziehung wirklich als eine gute Freundschaft, für die man unendlich
dankbar sein muss. Du weisst ja, hier verliert man jetzt viele Freunde,
oft in der erschütterndsten Weise, freilich man findet auch wieder viele.
Ich habe im letzten Jahre manche Menschen verloren, die mir wichtig waren
in meinem Leben, aber ich habe im Kampf der Kirche auch wieder eine Ge-
meinschaft gefunden, die nach menschlichem Ermessen unzerbrechlich ist.
Die Konturen werden ja immer klarer. Auch jetzt gerade wieder. Nur darum
muss man noch besorgt sein, dass man vor Einbrechen der Nacht weiss, wer
Freund ist und wer nicht. Dabei ist es gut zu wissen, dass auch drüben in

First page of final, typewritten letter of 27 March 1936.

# Afterword

## Wide, open spaces for service

Dietrich Bonhoeffer was as tireless in his desire to connect with young people as he was in seeking to connect devotional life to civic service. Wherever youthful aspiration thrived, he seized the opportunity to engage with the lives of young people and to invest in their ambitions and efforts. It seems that Bonhoeffer recognized that youth was a key stage in which to guide a person's creative energy, helping to foster whole living and spiritual development.[1] But to what end, if not to live out these life changes with integrity and in ways which were also productive and transforming?

This cache of letters to the teenager Ernst Cromwell, and the earlier theological discourse in this book, clearly confirm Bonhoeffer's relational approach to ministry. They reveal his awareness of the contribution of spirituality to personal change – the potential to affect not only other people but also socio-political structures and situations. Today, there is a timely opening for the Church[2] to

---

1 We are aware of UNCRC and other definitions of 'childhood', 'young people' and their age-related needs. The emphasis here is really on the malleable years of youthfulness, as opposed to full-blown maturity.

2 Calvin Van Reken's analysis is helpful in distinguishing between the Church as an 'institution' ('a unified organization') and as an 'organism' ('an aggregate of individual believers') in 'The Church's Role in Social Justice', a paper presented at the Calvin Theological Seminary (10 December 1998). The term 'Church' used here is

assess its work and its witness among young people, equipped as it is to encourage them in their lives, relationships and the wider social sphere. An encouraging comment to them would be: 'In being . . . *you will do.*'

In other words, presenting religious principles to young people under a 'Christianity' heading is simply inadequate. Spiritual modelling through practical lifestyle-coaching about the Christ-centred world view will help youth to own their spirituality and to explore hidden qualities within themselves.[3] Thus, the invitation is to pursue life purpose on a 'trek' with the most basic of prerequisites: the highest esteem for God, valuing of self, and valuing others (as one does oneself).In reviewing these letters one can imagine Bonhoeffer encouraging the Church today to welcome opportunities to engage with young people as if they were wide, open spaces – to connect with them in a renewed way. This is possible whether or not young people participate as members of a local worshipping community. In fact, it would be judicious to respond to the curiosity some may have about a higher power, about transcendence, about the historical Jesus and his salvation message for the twenty-first century. So, for example, a sense of vocation or personal 'call' to explore potential service roles within their own villages, cities and districts is a potentially helpful starting point.

Sometimes it seems that ubiquitous choice and the sheer range of lifestyle diversity and experiences will overwhelm our daily lives and challenge such local action. Yet, with appropriate support – whatever our age – choosing an area of service could mean a refreshed pedagogical approach to the outworking of faith in the twenty-first century. Linking faith, purpose and community responsibility may bring exciting discoveries towards more vibrant, self-aware and integrated

---

general, encompassing both dimensions. Unless otherwise stated, it is not limited to a specific geographical or national setting.

3   Nicholas Wolterstorff describes people's 'world view' as 'their way of thinking about life and the world, coupled with the values they set for themselves', in Brian J. Walsh and J. Richard Middleton, *The Transforming Vision: Shaping a Christian World View* (Downer's Grove, IL: IVP, 1984), pp. 9–10.

living. Put succinctly, exercising social responsibility could even bring surprising outcomes beyond the cash-strapped social service efforts of the state!

This 'connecting of dots', whereby we see that faith in Christ and his core message of salvation, justice and peace is fully applicable to relationships, work, rest and play, contrasts with the 'disembodied Christianity' bemoaned by contemporary American philosopher Nicholas Wolterstorff.[4] One wonders if this is a working theme throughout Bonhoeffer's short life. Admittedly, making these linkages requires a mindset which is outward-facing, one which leans closer to the ambition of 'good going viral', for service lived out *within church and the natural setting of the wider community.*

This raises questions about the Christ-centred world view and related youth programme activities of the Church: are these really perceived as adding value to the state and to society in general? If not, why so? If yes, by whom, and where is this effectively communicated and demonstrated, especially to young people?

These issues are acutely important for the public witness of the contemporary Church, and we may consider Bonhoeffer's London church at Sydenham as presenting a challenge for our times. The letters suggest congregational support for his youth outreach and confirmation classes in the 1930s. What are the appropriate efforts for neighbourhood churches within their own national and local settings today?

In commenting on American children who are exposed to community violence (as either victims or participants), Pastor and Professor of Religion David Corbin suggests: 'Rather than resort only to professionals who often live far away from the crime communities, what about Christian churches located in the heart of those communities?' He goes on: 'Despite the silence from the media, stories of conversion continue to come from pastors and Christian workers.

---

4    In this outstanding foundational book on the concept of world view by Walsh and Middleton, Wolterstorff makes introductory comments on the Judeo-Christian world view, in relation to everyday American life.

They are not only conducting funeral services for the victims of crime . . .'[5]

There is another dimension to world-view awareness which concerns twenty-first-century young people. It relates to their status as national and global citizens who may contribute to the public good as an expression of faith in Jesus Christ.[6] On this note of social responsibility at home and abroad, one question for the Church would be: 'How would this promote participatory governance within churches and new approaches to youth mission?'

Bonhoeffer must have struggled with similar questions in his lifetime, and it helps to remember that he was himself a young pastor when he penned these letters to the teenaged Ernst Cromwell. Despite this age factor, Bonhoeffer held fast to his faith and wrote with an understanding of the Church as it grappled with the nature of change in society. It is striking that, although he had a transforming vision for his time, it featured the following timeless elements:

- spiritual alertness – personal discipline which was clearly centred on his faith in Jesus Christ;
- gospel relevance – conviction that the gospel message was applicable to all aspects of life;
- purpose – a sense of self-awareness and personal call which was both significant and strategic (this may be considered as 'unction' but not to be confused with pride);[7]

---

5   Taken from 'MLK (Martin Luther King) and Non-Violence' at <http://monday-morning-minister.blogspot.com/2013/02/mlk-non-violence.html> 25 February 2013.

6   Jeremiah 29.5–7 is helpful here. This important reference is to biblical *shalom*, the defining salvation principle from which the Western concept of 'welfare' essentially evolved. Seeking 'shalom' in this instance would have meant conducting affairs mindful of the long-term wellbeing of individuals, community and the environment in which they lived. For an extensive study on this, see Perry B. Yoder, *Shalom: The Bible's Word for Salvation, Justice and Peace* (Nappanee, IN: Evangel Publishing House, 1987).

7   As the character 'M' advised James Bond: 'Arrogance and self-awareness seldom go hand in hand', in *Casino Royale* (Columbia Pictures Industries Inc., 2006). The Old Testament book of Proverbs already offers us an extensive study in the folly of pride.

- socio-political awareness – consciousness about the social problems of his day, the roles of Church and state, and the differentials of power within society;
- compelling engagement – commitment to friendship, with superb communication; serving others through his personal experience of faith and community;
- passion for everyday life and for liveliness.

In short, we can presume that Bonhoeffer understood life to be ministry, and service to be an aspect of worship. In his *Life Together* he issues sharp comments about the simple function of listening and acts of helpfulness:

> It is God's love for us that He not only gives us His Word but also lends us His ear. So it is His work that we do for our brother when we learn to listen to him . . .[8]

He wrote in this simple style to young Ernst, without hype or pretence.

Similarly, author Carol-Ann Morrow urges us to act out our faith in our times: 'We can have confidence that creation is unfolding according to God's will, but we can also help to make it so. Use your special gifts to bring kindness, peace and healing to a world in need.'[9] Morrow's message is blatantly practical and could well be a personalized memo for 'Generation Y' and other young people today. In contemporary terms, she promotes extending charity and demonstrating social responsibility *on Christ's behalf.*

We dare not reduce this to some impassioned call to become a teen-aged 'do-gooder'. The message is about doing good – deliberately and *on purpose* – with humility and in the 'company' of Christ.[10] Surely, this is still a faith stance within the high calling and mandate of the universal Church today!

---

8 From *Life Together*, in 'Catalog of the Exhibition' (Board of Bonhoeffer House, 1996), p. 68.

9 Carol-Ann Morrow, *Trust in God Therapy* (St Meinrad, IN: Abbey Press, 1998).

10 Matthew 28.20 and Ephesians 2.10 are encouraging references in this regard.

We may have this assurance when working to address complex problems such as gun violence and other crime, poverty, economic recession, child abuse, domestic violence, social exclusion and family breakdown. The good news is that any transformation vision for our neighbourhoods and districts is truly possible, and none is devoid of hope.

## Words on a page meaning influence and investment beyond time

All attempts at social change will eventually become unsustainable if they remain the exclusive business of adults. Bonhoeffer's devotional living style and engagement with young people could be instructive here. We should not underestimate the empowering role of friendship and mentoring as these relate to encouraging active youth citizenship. On this note, the London letters to Ernst Cromwell are essentially friendly letters. These documents present one side of a year-long 'conversation' between Bonhoeffer and Ernst. Apart from addressing some of Ernst's teenage concerns, they reveal rising socio-political commotion within Germany during the mid 1930s and the personal challenges that Bonhoeffer and his friends experienced.

With the benefit of hindsight, we now know that the Second World War would drastically affect the lives of both the letter writer and the recipient. Even so, their friendship held its own significance by featuring:

- the safety of parental awareness and other adult support;
- unconditional acceptance of the teenager;
- respect for the life experience of the mentor;
- respect for the age and learning status of the teenager;
- mutual trust, allowing discussion on a range of subjects (apart from matters of faith and devotional living);
- open attitudes to self-change (in both mentor and young person);
- some really good doses of fun!

Such secure bonds of friendship set no limits to what is achievable – even beyond age, space and time.[11]

It would be safe to assume from all this that Dietrich Bonhoeffer really did have some appreciation of how guiding friendships contributed to a young person's development. He might have also grasped that, despite the sincerest parental efforts at child-rearing, it takes time and some element of faith for a young person to believe, 'I am loved unconditionally'; 'I am unique and valuable'; 'I can make a difference to those around me.'[12] These could be incredible thoughts for anyone battling negative feelings of inadequacy, exploitation, abuse or social exclusion. They could also be life-changing thoughts for any young person benefiting from mentoring support, and we can envisage the potential changes when such thoughts are acted upon in homes, urban areas and other neighbourhoods in need of renewal. We can also help to make these changes happen . . .

Bonhoeffer's shared thoughts in the letters reveal practical influence and provide a motivating sway for the reader, towards reflection, self-awareness and personal development. Ernst gleaned lessons for life from these empowerment principles. He still reflects today on those times of Bible study many years ago and on treasured guidelines from the New Testament.[13]

This kind of letter writing is now being outpaced by instant electronic exercises, which do not require stamps and the vagaries of a national postal service. Some enthusiasts may assume that 'snail mail' is forever antiquated and obsolete. Others would prize letter mail as a more tangible and desirable form of correspondence, especially when it is a personal greeting.

---

11 At the time of writing, Ernest Edward Cromwell is now 92 years with a brilliant memory and still growing in grace and open to learning. He is not afraid to admit this. After reading Bonhoeffer's 1938 message to a confirmation group, he wrote, 'This now meant more to me aged 91 than it would have done when I was confirmed aged 14.'

12 Using a Christ-centred world view, one progression to this inner conversation would be, 'I can do all things through [Christ] who strengthens me' (Phil. 4.13).

13 Especially the Beatitudes and 1 Corinthians 13.

Perhaps this is because any serious decision to write (emails included) requires the ordering of thoughts. In the case of traditional letter writing, dependency on the passage of time enforces the discipline of waiting. This is an affront to the gratification of instant (or at least faster!) response. In the interim, it could help to enhance personal writing style, to nurture inner listening and reflection. We know it will take physical effort and commitment to respond in writing, and then the waiting begins again for the post. The time spans of snail mail can be tedious and are so unlike instant email.

Although some consider this an 'old-fashioned' way of doing things, traditional letter writing may yet help to prepare young minds for social dialogue and practical service to others,[14] quite possibly because it requires some projection away from self, a measure of focus on the recipient and, predictably, some waiting.

It is ironic that such qualities also ring true for volunteering and delivering other acts of service. The spiritual writer Richard Foster offers us some helpful thoughts on the productiveness of waiting. He says, 'Waiting is not something to be avoided at all costs. In waiting we learn things that we learn in no other way.'[15]

It is true that among young people Facebook, Twitter and email continue to make impressive headway in areas such as 'flash mobbing' and organizing mobile service groups. Assuming that there is some correlation between learning to 'wait' and learning to serve, traditional letter writing need not be completely abandoned for more instant communication. These may be complementary and together represent 'informal training' for any keen young person with an interest in what Bonhoeffer, in his *Life Together* (1939), calls 'outward acts of helpfulness'.

---

14 This is not an argument for 'backward thinking'. It is simply an acknowledgement of latent value in what might be considered passé. At the same time, there are new opportunities to mentor and support young people using ICT digital media systems (and in real time) which are open for exploration.

15 Richard J. Foster, in 'Waiting' taken from 'Heart to Heart' in the online magazine *Renovaré* (November 2007).

## Living out the friendship message

Bonhoeffer the letter writer chose his friendships well. He mixed with personalities such as Reinhold Niebuhr, Paul Lehmann and the Bishop of Chichester, George K. A. Bell. These associations flourished through visits, the exchange of correspondence, and lively debate. Overall, they made a lasting impression on his life. But in writing to Ernst on 27 March 1936, he refers to other people, unnamed but in his 'circle' of 'good friends, for whom one must forever be grateful.'

If friendship and networks were consistent themes which enabled this young pastor's work, it is not surprising that he employed this relational method in his writing and working with young people.[16] Almost 80 years have passed since the letters were written, yet Bonhoeffer's reflections and advice to young Ernst remain fresh and vibrant for our times. They reveal a relaxed pastoral manner that clearly connotes friendly influence and (one might even argue) some formative spiritual investment in the teenager's life. Thus, on the subject of friendship itself, Bonhoeffer writes soberly to Ernst on 27 March 1936:

> The only concern is to know, before night comes, who is a friend and who is not . . . I can tell you one thing: more important than any insight, than anything to do with your fundamental beliefs, is to have people in your life with whom you know that you share convictions.

Interestingly, terms such as 'fundamental beliefs' and 'convictions' are no longer easy banter today (especially to the Western mindset). These terms are sometimes used divisively or, at other times, perceived as expressing backward and self-righteous thinking. This particular 1936 letter reverberates with deeply held feelings and, perhaps, Bonhoeffer's own disappointment with failed alliances. It provides empowering

---

16 In 1931 he was elected to serve as an Honorary Youth Secretary in the 'World Alliance for Promoting Friendship through the Churches'. This organization had a Christian peace focus. See 'Catalog', p. 68.

advice for the young reader. If the writer's words could be reinterpreted (using the modern 'right to choose' approach), they would be suggesting a young person's 'right to choose friendships wisely'.

This is good advice whatever the place or century, but for young people today, making such choices could present an exercise in complexity. For some, one challenge would be prioritizing and selecting from among the instant (more abundant) versions of 'friends' now available via social media. Yet this is precisely the point about choice and learning to distinguish between those who are actually friends and those who are not . . . Bonhoeffer gave prudent counsel!

## 'Your faith today is a beginning, not a conclusion' – don't shout faith, just live it!

Ernst's confirmation in the Lutheran Church provided the original context for these letters and there are interesting questions about this important religious rite. Could Bonhoeffer have been implying some significance beyond a personal devotional exercise? When writing to the young confirmand, was he doing so reflectively or was he making a point that Ernst should know about the developments at home in Germany? These questions are worthy of note. Much of the letter writer's thoughts bear an urgent tone which matches the socio-political turbulence of the day. They expose the daily challenges to people of faith under Nazi rule in Germany.

Relating faith confession to daily life experience was once explained to a group of confirmands by the young pastor in this way:

> You do not have your faith once and for all. The faith that you will confess today with all your hearts needs to be regained tomorrow and the day after tomorrow, indeed, every day anew . . . Faith is the daily bread that God gives us . . . Your faith today is a beginning, not a conclusion.[17]

---

17  Sermon preached on 9 April 1938. Text quoted from Dietrich Bonhoeffer, *Theological Education Underground: 1937–1940* (DBWE), ed. Victoria J. Barnett; trans. Claudia D. Bergmann, Peter Frick and Scott A. Moore, Vol. 15 (Minneapolis: Fortress, 2012), Print. 476–80.

Although these words were spoken to a group of confirmands two years after the letters to Ernst of 1935/6, they echo the tone of that earlier correspondence. Bonhoeffer's words highlight the importance of developing an inner, devotional life as a basis for external acts of worship. From this viewpoint, Ernst's preparation and eventual confirmation in 1935 would have represented much more than a devout public declaration. This act would have been the beginning of a spiritual life quest to *walk faithfully*.

Moreover, a young person's public confession of faith and friendship with Christ could be the start of a holy mandate to serve others within the Church and the wider society in a myriad of ways.[18] From Bonhoeffer's perspective, as long as life continued, the 'conclusion' had not yet arrived and there was time to live out the faith walk.

When sharing these thoughts with young people today, the message is heartening. It presupposes no limits to what the redemptive lifestyle can accomplish, both within themselves and their communities. The journey is one of unending possibilities where faith in Christ could flourish under dedicated mentorship. Even the tests of human failings and inevitable conflicts can still help young women and men to mature.

In like spirit, on 20 March 1935 Bonhoeffer advises Ernst to be 'immeasurably happy that there is such a great cause as Christianity, which can use the help of each of us in some way. And be happy that whatever comes, we are not alone; we are in fellowship.' We can gather from this, and many thoughts shared, that the writer is acting from the seedbed of his own faith, not just as a friend and mentor to Ernst.

## All things connected and possible

It follows too that Bonhoeffer saw no dichotomy between faith and intelligent practice. Rather, we see him writing to Ernst as though

---

18  Bonhoeffer notes from his discussion, *The Church Facing the Jewish Question (April 1933)* 'The Church has an unconditional obligation to the victims of any ordering of society, even if they do not belong to the Christian community. Do good to all men . . .' – 'Catalog', p. 46.

matters of faith and spirituality related to *all* of life and not just to a separate category labelled 'religion'. Christian apologist Ravi Zacharias is persistent in exposing false separation and the so-called 'sacred–secular' divide which limits whole living today. He is candid in lamenting that 'Today, if faith is admitted at all, it is seen as the faith to have faith. It is packaged as a private matter and banned from intellectual credence.'[19]

Dietrich Bonhoeffer was clearly a thinking man of faith. It seems that his faith informed his living, and by his living he demonstrated his faith. Arguably, he did so to the point of death at the age of 39 in 1945. Prior to this, there was no dodging the central place of spirituality and the duty of servanthood in everyday life and affairs. There was no red or blue pill to take him down the rabbit hole![20] Bonhoeffer already lived in a reality which assumed the existence of the spirit world and the interconnection of all things. Furthermore, it was this salient truth that provided a backdrop for his teaching, for his work with young people, and for wider engagement with church and community.

We should note that anything was possible when the church 'community' was united. Therefore, Bonhoeffer writes in his inclusive tone to young Ernst on 8 June 1935 about the '*dunamis*' of spiritual fellowship:

> Spirit from above, Holy Spirit, mercy – truth from above, righteousness, courage – that is what we pray for . . . It is becoming more and more clear to me that everything will depend – in human terms – on forming such groups of people, who cannot be destroyed by any means in the world, and who allow themselves to be led by this Spirit. From afar, I count you as belonging to this group . . .

If these thoughts seem too impassioned, idealistic and otherworldly, the intent of the letters is sincere and still insightful for today.

---

19  Ravi Zacharias, *Jesus among Other Gods* (Nashville: Word Publishing, 2000), p. 57.
20  Reference here to 'Morpheus' speaking to 'Neo' (characters) in the film *The Matrix*, Warner Brothers Pictures (1999).

Ernst Cromwell

LONDON & NORTH EASTERN RAILWAY
CONTINENTAL SERVICES VIA HARWICH.
R.M.S. "PRAGUE"

10. Aug. 1935 *

*Lieber Kurt !*

Letter written on RMS *Prague*, 13 August 1935

Sometimes Bonhoeffer refers to lifestyle challenges and social problems which are current difficulties in our times. For example, we see him commenting on a range of topics from hospitality to racism in the mid 1930s. These include the so-called 'Jewish issue', the benefits of true friendship, stress and work–life balance, censorship and political oppression, the power of economic interests, and religiosity. He complains about stressful travel and the quirks of maritime Channel crossing in 1935.[21] Bonhoeffer even hints about contrived government policy to accommodate the 1936 Berlin Olympics.

On the other hand, this letter writer discusses the virtues of practising community – the personal and collective gains of members, and their inescapable trials. The correspondence is replete with themes of participation, group effort, togetherness and the 'circle' that are sociologically fascinating. There are many references to the Cromwell household (and to Ernst's obligations there) and even guidance for cordial debate with a zealous religious teacher!

In 1935, the writer makes an ominous reference to the social upheaval in Germany (and the unspeakable pressures which would follow) when he states poetically,

> We are under the impression that the path we are taking is soon going to lead us into serious disputes. This is not so hard as long as we are together here, but at some point we shall leave here to live separately, each standing on his own. Then will come the time of waiting it out, of seeing it through, which already strikes fear into every heart.[22]

In spite of this, Dietrich Bonhoeffer remains positive and counsels Ernst about the difference true friendship makes in times of distrust and when things are falling apart. But it was not a case of 'all work and no play'. Bonhoeffer mentions festival days, enjoyment of food, sports, other hobbies and delights. These are all things which we enjoy with

---

21  He acknowledges the medicinal value of a shot of whisky to combat this unpleasant experience!

22  Letter from Germany to Ernst Cromwell, London, 20 November ('Repentance Day') 1935.

Ernest E. Cromwell at the age of 92, December 2012

friends and family and, in his own words on 27 March 1936, they are among 'the few things in life that are really important and that make life worth living.'

Although we do not have the benefit of reading Ernst's written responses, some elements in the letters must have captured his daily life as a teenager and would have encouraged him at that stage of his development. Above all this, the mentor counselled Ernst not to 'forget the time of your confirmation'. Many decades of religious and other life experiences have passed, and even after 78 years, he has not forgotten!

## Kingdom citizenship and earthly responsibility

But why all these observations and details entrusted to a 14-year-old boy? Did the writer believe that the status of citizenship (whether heavenly or earthly) was not solely the reserve of adults? If so, this would not have been novel thinking. Back in the first century, Jesus Christ made a deliberate, if mysterious, connection between the kingdom of God and childlikeness. He equated childlikeness and humility with 'greatness'. These were among Christ's primary standards for citizenship in *his* kingdom and, presumably, for living and working devotionally.[23]

In like manner, the letters show an appreciation for the tenderness of youth but also for the latent potential within young people. We get the impression that youth citizenship and responsible service are definitely validated. Even by Bonhoeffer's own demonstration, the connection between the themes of active faith and the civic participation of young people (in the interest of others) is obvious.[24]

---

23  This astounding statement is recorded in Matthew 18.1–6. For more on this topic, we can refer to Dr Keith White's extensive work in the Child Theology Movement and, particularly, his paper entitled 'A Little Child Will Lead Them' <www.childtheologymovement.org/new/articles>.

24  Bonhoeffer reflects in his 8 June 1935 letter to Ernst, 'So you see that the work here is very satisfying and fulfilling, and indeed makes each of us happy, even though it often does not come without considerable renunciation for a while. I believe and hope also that in this way we are performing a real service to the Church and to Germany . . .'

As a result of this, we could imagine Bonhoeffer making a case today for the greater participation of young people in national governance and international development concerns. However, this would be the type of participation which does not serve political oppression and other dark agendas.

It is true that this 'participation' terminology is modern policy jargon and anachronistic to Dietrich Bonhoeffer's time period. However, the young pastor was already living out some aspects of participation. We may interpret this in his own planning and strategizing, preaching, teaching, leadership attendance at national and international conferences, along with copious 'reporting' to young people like Ernst and to many other friends.

On the international scene, Bonhoeffer was sociologically curious and clearly hated injustice. He was anxious to learn about citizens' movements which addressed socio-political oppression. These included the prejudice and institutional discrimination faced by the black population in Harlem during the early 1930s. His voluntary efforts within the Church and community during these times provided a striking contrast with the xenophobic national service (such as the 'Hitler Youth') that was later introduced in Germany.

We have already heard from the earlier narrative on Ernest's testimony that Bonhoeffer spoke with him about wanting to meet with Mahatma Gandhi. He was keen to learn more about the alternative peace movement in India. It seems that Bonhoeffer was driven by a constant alertness to the significance of the times in which he lived and, in this regard, he made every effort to share and to work closely with young people such as Ernst Cromwell.

His mentoring approach was sometimes very bold too. It revealed a sweeping (if not deliberate) assumption that the teenager was interested in the socio-political concerns of Church and state. Thus, he writes in late March 1936 (just days before Ernst's fifteenth birthday) about the difficult and dangerous times: 'I haven't heard from you personally in a long time. But I think you still understand what I am saying.'

Was he indicating in some way that this information would be instructive to Ernst in the future?[25] If so, it is intriguing that the statements show the forward-looking and trusting nature of Bonhoeffer's faith. Our letter writer was remarkably ahead of his time and later, in 1938, we see progression in his inclusive thinking about the civic responsibility of the young, socially aware worshipper. He addresses the confirmation class of that year: 'Your "Yes" to God demands your "No" to all injustice, to all evil, to all lies, to all oppression and violation of the weak and poor, to all godlessness and mocking of the Holy.'

Being included and treated as an 'insider' can still boost confidence and become an empowering experience for many a teenager. Ernst was no different in 1936 when 15 years old and he easily recalls today that the emphasis then was on building character.

## Still anyone's call . . .

As far as Bonhoeffer was concerned, this business of faith, civic duty and international awareness was a weighty issue, and he was watchful and vigilant about the times in which he lived. As a mentor to Ernst, it seems as though he deliberately invested thoughts for the years ahead. Again, he writes in 1936,

> What is crucial for you, in these quiet years that are still given to you, is to find and acquire the powers and the energy that you will need some day, in different times. And again, the most important thing is to hold fast to the truth, and not to let anything else influence you.[26]

In reality, we no longer live in 'quiet years', and there are many children and teenagers today whose lives are troubled and turbulent for

---

25  Ernest now reflects that he really was not absorbed in politics at that time. Yet we should note in his interview that, despite the difficult internment which he and his family suffered in England as German refugees, his sense of civic duty was fully intact. He still went on to serve as a wartime captain among the British troops fighting against the Nazis and the Axis powers.

26  Letter of 27 March 1936.

a host of negative reasons. It is because of this that, while providing the necessary 'practical' support for young people, the deeper issues of spirituality and faith must not be neglected. These provide young people with access to a world view – essential values and principles which serve as a foundation for living. Failing this, how could contemporary notions of 'young people's wellbeing' be considered truly efficient?

Acknowledging young people's participation is now unfolding social policy and a growing trend in both national and global development programmes. In countries such as the UK the structures of national state institutions, the services of non-governmental organizations, planning, budgeting and other operations are only now catching up with certain aspects of this thrust. The message seems to be: 'We do not have to wait for young people to become the "leaders of tomorrow" as their contributions are already valuable today.'

The Council of Europe is implementing a similar approach in its 2012–15 strategy, which deems it 'essential that children are involved in its work on children's rights'.[27] The participation agenda is also expanding to the international financial sector where initiatives such as the Child and Youth Finance International (CYFI) movement are engaging with young people. The main intention here is to address problems of poverty, youth unemployment, abuse, lack of health care and other vulnerabilities, through the financial education of children and young people.[28]

Also in recent times, this momentum for youth civic engagement is gaining powerful advocates. On the most recent 'National Day of Service' in the USA, President Obama commented on young Americans in volunteerism and civic duty. He was clearly pleased about the overwhelming response to this special day as an indication of 'huge hunger on the part of young people to get involved and to get engaged'.[29]

---

27  As presented at the Grimaldi Forum, Monaco (20–21 November 2011).

28  To date, CYFI has delivered its message to 18,738,224 young people worldwide. See webpage at <http://childfinance international.org>.

29  President Barack Obama – these comments were shared on 19 January 2013 <http://news.msn.com/politics/americans-turn-out-for-national-day-of-service/>.

It would prove an interesting sociological enquiry to find out what percentage of these young people were either members of faith communities, took part because of faith-related convictions or were somehow encouraged by others with such convictions. Whatever the case, it is this youthful desire for engagement and association with something meaningful that needs to be channelled and supported appropriately.

With regard to the arts and cultural expression, internationally renowned film director Steven Spielberg has made a valid case for youth participation through a special video project to 'encourage youngsters to do more for their communities'. In his presentation to a gathered audience, Spielberg advised that 'Acts of kindness do not always have to be random'.[30]

This 'new' thrust towards 'young people's participation' is enlightening and exciting. Yet it is worth noting that much of this thrust already has a biblical precedent, one which *always* valued childhood and youth. Indeed, some aspects of this approach have been faithfully adopted by churches and other groups in their diverse multicultural settings. But who can really show and tell consistently at any national levels? The matter is still to be fully owned, explored and addressed within the Church itself.

With this in mind, the following questions may provide a helpful assessment for local churches and associations at both national and international levels:

- In view of Christ's mandate to 'preach', 'teach', 'feed' and 'heal', what is the status of young people's participation in delivering this much-needed gospel?
- How does this participation approach affect the current teaching, training, leadership and mentoring, prayer networks and

---

30  Refer to <http://www.youtube.com/watch?v=lZb9t_Lk380>. The 'I Witness Video Challenge' initiative is administered by the University of Southern California Shoah Foundation which works closely with students and other young people. International goals include using the testimonies of genocide survivors from places such as Rwanda and Darfur.

other business-planning systems within local faith communities (including faith-based services)?

- In what ways does this youth participation message affect the specific governance structures within churches and the potential for appropriate inter-generational leadership?
- How do the views of so-called 'non-churched' youth inform the work of local churches?
- Where individual churches are already implementing changes in this arena, how are these activities being recorded, monitored and reported, and to whom? Moreover, how are they further enhanced through prophetic leadership?
- Where the Church (at the national/international level) is making strides in these areas, how is any added value being understood and recorded within geographical settings by the state, the media and by other faith communities?

These are poignant questions directly linked to the larger topic of faith-based service as part of the Church's heritage and ongoing cross-cultural mission. This awaits dedicated academic research and social assessment at both national and international levels. For example, the following commentary was recently made about faith-based organizations on the African continent: '[These groups are] critical constituent elements of social development' and 'Arguably therefore, besides ethnicity, faith is a significant variable influencing governance, conflict, and the nature of the African nation-state'.[31]

The Church in the West is not short of examples where funds and people (among other resources) have advanced the wellbeing of children and youth, both at home and globally.[32] Contributions for donor

---

31  As expressed in the general abstract for the International Society for Third Sector Research (ISTR), Africa Civil Society Research Network Conference. This event is planned for 11–13 July 2013 in Nairobi, Kenya.

32  The emerging concept of Social Return on Investment (SROI) can make a significant contribution to this arena. It introduces the possibility of measurement to non-financial programme areas in development work which were previously undervalued or simply deemed unquantifiable. Refer to the New Economics Foundation in London for more cutting-edge research on SROI, applied to community projects.

aid, and actual programme delivery to support young people and international development efforts, are also worth noting. Added to these would be the enduring charity and community service that is characteristic of most church work, even when other efforts, resources and partnerships fail.

In the case of the UK and other Western nations, up-to-date enquiry on this topic and the ensuing social and other returns for the state should provide a revealing socio-economic study. This is particularly important in the midst of austerity measures to meet economic recession and promote welfare reform.

It would also be significant if that exercise noted specific initiatives for young people and categories of other church-based community work. Apart from funding contributions, these would include historical precedent in promoting charity work and the originality of genuine 'not for profit' status; nurturing and providing local access to indigenous knowledge and management systems, intellectual property in programme innovation and instructional design; and provision of infrastructure (including access to networks and real estate).

## Forward ever . . .

Perhaps the overall significance of Bonhoeffer's 'letters to London' is that they could have been addressed to any teenager in most neighbourhoods and cities today. They could have been written to any young person wrestling with issues of faith, life purpose and growing up. Although the correspondence was set in a historical timeframe, the letters still possess a timeless, international appeal.

The writer's outreach style may yet encourage us in daily service to an eternally relevant, multicultural Christ. This approach is likely to affect internal review and current concepts of 'church', how the Church is perceived by others, and, how the Church actually 'does' church. In practical terms, it should include making appropriate institutional changes for the full participation of young people in the Church's mission today.

On the wider front, the time is ripe for forms of social policy, development theory, ethical business and other praxis that fully acknowledge spirituality and faith as core aspects of being human. Thus, these would be also latent resource areas for addressing social problems and for enabling social and economic wellbeing in society. Relativism may now be in vogue, but by its very nature relativism will inevitably frustrate the notion of 'values' and any basis for determining what is truly valuable.

The motivation for action need not be about 'Christianity' – in whatever shade, brilliance or fashion – or even the distraction of religious debate. Rather, a contemporary case for revisiting the values of the historical Jesus to inform life today is both logical and feasible. It is especially pertinent in instances where references to the 'Christian heritage' of a particular cause or nation are made. In such instances, should this not be appropriately revisited and any profits gleaned?

In terms of moving forward, reference to a Christ-centred world view can help to make young people fit for their life purpose and for civic service, when this perspective allows opportunity to:

- acknowledge their 'inner world', thus contributing to their overall potential for wellbeing;[33]
- embrace a comprehensive belief system about purpose in life and a cognitive basis for values;
- provide support for the young person's development of self-worth and for respecting and valuing all others;
- contribute to the daily motivation 'powers and energy' (solace, strategy and hope) of the young person;
- demonstrate social return on investment (SROI) to the state, especially where the young person is afforded the civil right of living out their own values, in ways which help to enhance the lives of

---

33 For insightful research on this concept of young people's wellbeing, see *Backing the Future: Why Investing in Children Is Good for Us All*, an Action for Children and New Economics Foundation Report (2009).

others and which clearly benefit the state (e.g. practising neigh-bourly as opposed to anti-social behaviour).

Dietrich Bonhoeffer was very upfront about faith as an indispensable resource for personal development and daily life. In these 'letters to London', he was candid about this and about his relationship with 'Jesus Christ, whom we confess'.[34] It would be inconsistent to admire the ethical thinking of Bonhoeffer the man, while spurning the central figure behind his ethical message.

Today, the confession statement is still anyone's call. It holds endless possibilities for young people who are keen to participate and to get involved in civic service. It holds special promise for young people who – like Dietrich Bonhoeffer – are not afraid to demonstrate that just as faith without works is dead, ethics without faith is naked.

*Toni Burrowes-Cromwell*

---

34  Letter of 27 March 1936.

# References

## Books, papers and reports

Action for Children and New Economics Foundation Report, *Backing the Future: Why Investing in Children Is Good for Us All* (2009).

Barnett, Victoria J. (ed.), *Dietrich Bonhoeffer, Theological Education Underground: 1937–1940* (DBWE, Vol. 15), trans. Claudia D. Bergmann, Peter Frick and Scott A. Moore (Minneapolis: Fortress Press, 2012).

Foster, Richard J., 'Waiting', taken from 'Heart to Heart' in *Renovaré*, online magazine (November 2007).

*Life Together*, in 'Catalog of the Exhibition' (Board of Bonhoeffer House, 1996).

Morrow, Carol-Ann, *Trust in God Therapy* (St Meinrad, IN: Abbey Press, 1998).

Van Reken, Calvin, 'The Church's Role in Social Justice', paper presented at the Calvin Theological Seminary (10 December 1998).

Walsh, B. and Middleton, R., *The Transforming Vision: Shaping a Christian World View* (Downer's Grove, IL: InterVarsity Press, 1984).

Yoder, Perry B., *Shalom: The Bible's Word for Salvation, Justice and Peace* (Nappanee, IN: Evangel Publishing House, 1987).

Zacharias, Ravi, *Jesus among Other Gods* (Nashville: Word Publishing, 2000).

Zimmermann, D. and Smith, G. (eds), *I Knew Dietrich Bonhoeffer* (London: Collins Fontana, 1973).

## Conferences

Abstract for the International Society for Third Sector Research (ISTR) at the Africa Civil Society Research Network Conference: event originally planned for 11–13 July 2013 in Nairobi, Kenya.

Council of Europe, Strategy for 2012–2015 concerning children's rights, presented to the Grimaldi Forum, Monaco (20–21 November 2011).

**Films**

*Casino Royale* (Columbia Pictures Industries Inc., 2006).
*The Matrix* (Warner Brothers Pictures, 1999).

**Websites**

Anderson, R., *Ten Theses on Dietrich Bonhoeffer: Theologian, Christian, Martyr* (2007). Available at <http://www.faith-theology.com/2007/06/ten-theses-on-dietrich-bonhoeffer.html>.

Biblical Discernment Ministries, *Dietrich Bonhoeffer: General Teachings/Activities* (2010). Available at <http://www.rapidnet.com/~jbeard/bdm/exposes/bonhoeffer/general.htm>.

Bouma, Jake, *The Lost Confirmation Sermon of Dietrich Bonhoeffer* (2012). Available at <http://www.jakebouma.com/dietrich-bonhoeffer-confirmation-sermon/>.

Children and Youth Finance International (CYFI) at <http://childfinance international.org>.

Corbin, David, 'MLK (Martin Luther King) and Non-Violence' (25 February 2013). Available at <http://mondaymorning-minister.blogspot.com/2013/02/mlk-non-violence.html>

'I Witness Video Challenge' at <http://www.youtube.com/watch?v=lZb9t_Lk380>, administered by the University of Southern California Shoah Foundation.

Obama, Barack (19 January 2013) at <http://news.msn.com/politics/americans-turn-out-for-national-day-of-service/>.

White, Keith, 'A Little Child Will Lead Them'. Available at <www.childtheologymovement.org/new/articles>.

# Index